Yale Historical Publications, Miscellany, 115

Americans and German Scholarship 1770-1870

Carl Diehl

New Haven and London
Yale University Press
1978

Published under the direction of the Department of History of Yale
University with assistance from the income of the Frederick John
Kingsbury Memorial Fund.

Poem 745 by Emily Dickinson, copyright 1929 by Martha Dick-
inson Bianchi; © 1957 by Mary L. Hampson. Reprinted from
The Complete Poems of Emily Dickinson, edited by Thomas H.
Johnson, by permission of Little, Brown and Co.

*Designed by Thos. Whitridge
and set in IBM Selectric Press Roman type.
Printed in the United States of America by Vail-Ballou Press,
Binghamton, New York.*

*Published in Great Britain, Europe, Africa, and Asia (except Japan)
by Yale University Press, Ltd., London. Distributed in Latin
America by Kaiman & Polon, Inc., New York City; in Australia and
New Zealand by Book & Film Services, Artarmon, N.S.W.,
Australia; and in Japan by Harper & Row, Publishers, Tokyo Office.*

Library of Congress Cataloging in Publication Data

*Diehl, Carl, 1947–
    Americans and German scholarship, 1770–1870.*

    *(Yale historical publications: Miscellany; 115)
    Based on the author's thesis, Yale.
    Bibliography: p.
    Includes index.
    1. American students in Germany–History. 2. College students–
United States. 3. College students–Germany. I. Title. II. Series.
LA721.7.D53   378.1'98   77–12931
ISBN 0-300-02079-1*

To my mother and father

Πρῶτον μὲν οὖν τοὺς παλαιοὺς χινδύνους τῶν
προγόνων δίειμι, μνήμην παρὰ τῆς φήμης λαβών.

[First, I will recount the ancient dangers of
our ancestors, taking my record from tradition.]

—Lysias, II.2

Contents

Renunciation—is a piercing Virtue—
The letting go
A Presence—for an Expectation—
Not now—
The putting out of Eyes—
Just Sunrise—
Lest Day—
Day's Great Progenitor—
Outvie
Renunciation—is the Choosing
Against itself—
Itself to justify
Unto itself—
When larger function—
Make that appear—
Smaller—that Covered Vision—Here—

—Emily Dickinson
Poem 745

Preface

The crisis of historicism, that mordant and melancholy subversion of the nineteenth-century historical imagination, has captured the attention of intellectual historians and literary critics. Belatedness, the lament of the latecomer for his own lack of priority in the historical process, is traced backward from Nietzsche's dark, ostentatious ironies and well-advertised Weltschmerz to the sunnier strategies of Hegel and Herder. And belatedness might indeed be found on every page of Herder—defeated by that power of celebration which defined its own historical and literary authenticities.

Herder was not a philologist; but he signals the birth of a new historical philology, even as Nietzsche announces its death. Between them stretches a curious nineteenth-century scholastic corpse, a shamanism of the word which H. S. Chamberlain and Alfred Rosenberg tricked us into forgetting. This is Nietzsche's final victory over his teachers, Heyne, Wolf, Boeckh, and Ritschl: we have forgotten even their names. Thus Hayden White, contrasting the "deep structure of the historical imagination" with Kuhn's model of scientific discovery, remarks, in *Metahistory: The Historical Imagination in Nineteenth-Century Europe* (Baltimore, 1973):

The physical sciences appear to progress by virtue of the agreements, reached from time to time among members of the established community of scientists, regarding what will count as a scientific problem, the form that a scientific explanation must take, and the kinds of data that will be permitted to count as evidence in a properly scientific account of reality. Among historians no such agreement exists, or has ever existed. [p. 13]

But only by a severe limitation of the term "historians" can the last statement be true. For there developed throughout the nineteenth century communities of scholars in history and the other disciplines of the humanities with broad but defined criteria regarding what would count as a scholarly problem, the form that a scholarly explanation should take, and the kinds of data that would be permitted to count as evidence in a properly scholastic account of reality. Moreover, these communities and their criteria developed long before the physical sciences could offer a model of organization or values.

The first modern problem of history or the humanities, as I attempt to illustrate in my second chapter, is the Homeric question, defined by late eighteenth-century German classical philology. The historical analysis of language was brought to bear on literary and historical data with spectacular results. Historical vision transposed into philological technique became the crucial methodological breakthrough of modern scholarship. And in defining its own problems and the criteria for evidence and solutions, modern scholarship in the humanities defined itself. The agreement which White so casually denies underlies all of Humboldt's reforms and his enshrinement of philology as the capstone of humanistic education in the nineteenth century.

Philology, the half-brother of historicism, matured rapidly. Beyond the Homeric question, the immense puzzle of languages and language itself beckoned. Like another intellectual monument of the nineteenth century, the theory of biological evolution, the ancient secrets of linguistic evolution lay hidden, almost-discovered, waiting for their Darwin and Wallace. More vividly than the Homeric question, Indo-European philology defined the modern scholar as the solver of puzzles, and his discipline as the definition of self-evolving puzzles. Vocation was implicit in vision, the power to create problems and be seduced by them.

The victory of technique (in Jacques Ellul's sense) was rapid and complete. In the space of a single generation, from Herder to Humboldt, it triumphed. In Humboldt's elevation of Wolf as the model for his new University of Berlin there is a kind of suicide of humanism, a humanism for which Nietzsche, the last philologist, mourned.

The crisis of historicism, however, passed unnoticed in nineteenth-century American scholarship. Twentieth-century American scholars have not bothered to ask why, the answer seems so obvious. Yet, hundreds and perhaps thousands of Americans had been trained in the same methods and inculcated with the same criteria as Nietzsche. They, too, followed in the path of Wolf, Boeckh, and Ritschl—or at least they appeared to. Why did they not go through that crisis? If they had learned the same things in the same places as the Europeans, if they had adopted the same vision and the same vocation, why did they not go through what the Europeans went through?

These are curious questions; and I cannot pretend to answer them. But they indicate how little is known of the evolution of modern scholarship in the humanities and the "agreements" and criteria which underlie it. The following work attempts only to sketch one small part of that process: the acquisition of technique and the rejection of vision by Americans who studied in German universities. It is intended only as a beginning, and if it stimulates more fruitful and accurate efforts, it will have been as successful as I could wish.

Several years ago, in an unguarded moment which I am sure he may already have had cause to regret, my dissertation adviser, R. R. Palmer, complained of the length and turgidity of modern Ph.D. dissertations and invited more speculative—and shorter—efforts. I hope that, in those respects at least, that thesis and this book which grew out of it have fulfilled some of his expectations.

Introduction

Both the form and the content of modern American scholarship in the humanities owe their initial and principal debt to the great migration of American students to German universities throughout the nineteenth century. Between nine and ten thousand Americans—a large proportion of them in the humanities and social sciences—crossed the ocean to study. As Jurgen Herbst remarks, "The magnitude of this transatlantic migration would be sufficient to arouse the historian's interest even if he were not immediately concerned with the consequences entailed for the development of American education."[1]

It was a complex and extensive debt. The Americans derived not only the structure of academic scholarship from their studies in Berlin and Göttingen, but their very conception of what scholarship was and how it should be pursued. To quote Herbst again:

It was from blueprints drawn after the German academic pattern, transported across the ocean by these scholars and many of their compatriots, that the ground was prepared for a successful reorganization of American institutions of higher education.[2]

The word *blueprints* is misleading. Americans could not, and most did not wish, merely to copy the German forms and institutions. They learned from the Germans, but often with a great deal of difficulty, and rarely, in any case, what the Germans taught at any one moment. A simple comparison of German and American works of scholarship will show similarities and "influences." But the distinctions are always clear.

Moreover, German scholarship itself was in a process of evolution throughout the nineteenth century. And it became increasingly split between its ideals and practice throughout the century. The glorious humanistic purpose which Humboldt had bequeathed his University of Berlin persisted in the rhetoric of his successors (as it persists today). But these ideals had less and less to do with what actually transpired in the library

1

and lecture halls of the Frederick William or Georgia Augusta. And even when this high-flown rhetoric of a unitary humanistic education appealed to many of the Americans, most of them could not even understand, let alone transpose, much of that.

The "influence," then, was not a simple one. Yet its very complexity can tell us a great deal about the evolution of modern academic scholarship in the humanities. There is already a large body of historical literature on some aspects of the migration of American students to Germany, primarily on the first few: George Ticknor, Edward Everett, George Bancroft, and Joseph Green Cogswell. But there are essentially two flaws in most of this work. First, virtually every historian of these men fails to perceive how little each of them learned in Germany, how hard it was for them to acquire what they did, and how little of that resembled the advanced work of the German scholars of the day. Almost every one of Bancroft's biographers remarks wistfully on how little Bancroft was able to impart to Harvard and Boston on his return, and to a man they ascribe the blame for this to Boston or Harvard. Yet, when Bancroft had ample leisure and opportunity to pursue his own studies as he wished he did not better; his brand of scholarship was certainly far from the German standard to which he had been exposed. And the same is true of other great German-trained historians like J. L. Motley.

The second failing of the existing historical literature on the American migration abroad is that it greatly exaggerates the influence of the first students in the making of the institutions of American higher education. Although many of these first students who returned from Germany attained some influence in American education, they did surprisingly little with their power. Certainly, Edward Everett, as president of Harvard, could have accomplished far more than he did. Perhaps the greatest achievement of these first four American students was Cogswell's collection of the Astor Library, the first advanced research library in the United States. But that was done for a private patron outside the existing structure of American higher education. It, like virtually every other achievement of these first migrants, could provide at best only an isolated example for later reformers.

If the Americans did not pick the German learning like fruit from a tree, what difference did that make? Why bother finding out what their difficulties were and how they solved them? There are essentially two reasons. First, by tracing the experience of the Americans in German universities we can infer what they actually learned there. Their own summaries and notes do not provide this information because they tell us only what classes the Americans attended, not what they actually absorbed. The Americans, if they did not absorb everything—or even very much—did learn something, and it is crucial for understanding the subsequent development of higher education in this country to learn more precisely what. Second, the psychological difficulties which the Americans encountered might shed some light on whether there are psychological and social criteria for modern scholarship in the humanities as well as intellectual ones, and if so, what these might be.

The institutional history of the modern university in Germany has been brilliantly explored by Steven Turner.[3] But there is as yet no satisfactory intellectual history of the development of modern scholarship within that university. One of the greatest difficulties in writing such a history is the continuity of German scholarship—especially classical philology—throughout the eighteenth century and into the nineteenth. But the study of the experiences of American students in German universities provides an example of near-perfect discontinuity. Except for the smallest handful among them, the Americans did not have an inkling of the kind of scholarship that awaited them. And their attempts to come to terms with it give the historian a valuable insight into not only the power and meaning of the modern form of scholarship, but the price which had to be paid for that scholarship.

What did the Americans learn in Germany? Most of the students of the humanities when they enrolled in a university studied philology, which is to say that most of them studied classical languages and literatures from a historical point of view. It would be gratifying to be able to be more specific than that. Unfortunately, the Germans themselves tended to be rather less so, if anything. What the Americans really seemed to do in the seminars was to study the language of the classical texts in such a way as to reveal not only the historicity of the particular work, but, with the help of the proper interpretation of the content, to give a historical insight into the society, values, and world-view of the author. In contrast to the often moribund teaching of American colleges, the Germans would also not disdain to use every other source of historical knowledge to illuminate the meanings of texts, as well as to arrive at a better understanding of the composition and the circumstances surrounding the composition and transmission of the manuscripts. Although many Americans tried their hand at some kind of etymological study while they were in the philological seminars, very few of them progressed from relatively simple techniques to the kind of analysis of the historical evolution of languages and language groups which was the major achievement of German scholars in the first half of the nineteenth century.

What was new to Americans about the kind of study described above was not only the study of literary texts in their entirety (a practice not general in American colleges of the day), but a historical insight which we may now take for granted but which offered a fresh authenticity to both Germans and Americans. For Germans there were many social and institutional aids to fan that sense of authenticity into a commitment to a life of scholarship. But for Americans throughout the first three-quarters of the century, there were almost no such aids. Scholarship for Americans was European; but it was not just a European "idea" in the casual sense of that word. For it implied a sense of vocation which demanded to be felt and made into a specifically American thing.

The "research ideal" is yet another of these glib phrases. But that, too, implies the same thing. And the commitment that it demanded was considerably more than the older ideals of American education: discipline, piety, utility, liberal culture, to use Lawrence Veysey's categories. "Aspiring Americans who visited Germany and came back with the phrase 'scientific research' on their lips," had to go through a great deal before they could embrace that ideal. If they "compounded the phrase from elements which had very different contexts in their original habitat,"[4] that was psychologically and socially necessary.

To dedicate one's life to the pursuit of knowledge implies only a personal commitment. But for a large number of people, to do so implies that status, economic security, institutions—in other words, the forces of social commitment—are at work. Thus, to the extent that scholarship requires enough practitioners for specialization as well as an institutional structure, it also requires a specifically social value. And part of the history of scholarship in America is the history of its growing acceptance among the social elite.

The gradual evolution of this sense of personal and social commitment to the scholarly vocation is the theme of this book. The first chapter gives a sketch of the ideal of scholarship, or at least the rhetoric of scholarship, that Americans encountered in Germany. The chapter tries to convey the sense of discovery and excitement that was generated by philological investigations into Greek language and literature. The implications for academic scholarship of the particular nationalistic and historical concerns of those decades are also discussed. The second chapter centers on one individual, F. A. Wolf, not because of what he personally taught Americans (for he met only a handful and taught none), but because of the way in which he shaped the insights of his predecessors into a paradigm of academic research. In the third chapter I examine the migration of American students to Germany in the first seven decades of the nineteenth century. The chapter delineates where they came from, where and what they studied, and what they did after their return to America. The fourth chapter concentrates on how the first Americans to study in Germany perceived this new form of scholarship and on their inability to assimilate it. It focuses on their psychological difficulties in forming a commitment to the new scholarship. The following chapter explores the growing social and intellectual acceptance in America of the new form of learning. Finally, I return to Germany to depict the ways in which a later generation of American students were able to overcome the psychological difficulties that had stymied their precursors and transport a truly modern form of scholarship to America.

CHAPTER 1

As in a high valley repeated avalanches have built a thick roof of old yellow snow and the torrent flows in a choked stream many metres below, so the accretions of the professional mind require removal before we can contemplate the source.

This simile applies to the whole study of classical antiquity, but pre-eminently to that of Homer, where the development of theory during the nineteenth century will provide the future psychologist with strange data for the study of the aberration of the intellect.

—T. W. Allen,
The Origin and Transmission of Homer

In the second half of the eighteenth century, in the period of classical German literature, a new humanism frees itself and begins to stand on its own feet; it has a totally different stamp, and a far greater breadth and depth than Renaissance humanism.

—Ernst Cassirer,
The Logic of the Humanities

Choked Streams:
The Rhetorical Theology of
Neuhumanistische Philology

When in 1815 George Ticknor and Edward Everett exchanged the provincial security of Boston for exotic and arduous labors at Göttingen, they had little idea of the intellectual experience that awaited them. Ticknor confessed to a little reluctance at the thought of the journey:

The prospect of the pleasures and profits of a voyage to Europe and of travelling there, grows dim and sad as I approach it. One who, like myself, has always been accustomed to live, in the strictest sense of the phrase, *at home,* and never to desire any pleasures which could not be found there,—one who has had never enough of curiosity to journey through his own country,—can hardly feel much exultation at the prospect of being absent two or three years from that country in which all his wishes and hopes rest as in their natural center and final home.[1]

Once settled, the two Americans maintained a large correspondence with friends and relatives at home. Their letters, as might be expected, are full of the fabulous minutiae of German university life: duels, beer-drinking students, and seedy professors with their homes, wives, and children. The university quickly impressed them and they said so. The library, the lecture and seminar systems, the freedom—all these they appreciated and praised highly. But it was not the external institutions, facilities, customs that attracted their greatest attention. Their awe was reserved for the scholarship which all of these supported. They valued the German academic system less for what it was then for what it produced.

German scholarship seemed to them as different from the leisurely pursuits of an American gentleman such as Thomas

Jefferson (whom Ticknor had visited just before leaving for Germany) as Harvard College was from Göttingen. As Ticknor said later of Germany:

Indeed, the business of education, I believe, is better understood there and more thoroughly carried on, than anywhere else;—as, in truth, seems to be plainly enough proved by the fact that there are more really learned men and there is absolute learning in Germany, than in all the rest of the world.[2]

It was not just a difference in amount of learning but in kind. Ticknor, describing to his father what he had found in Göttingen, called the German universities a "Republic of letters."[3] This may have been a common figure of speech in Jeffersonian America; but Ticknor meant it almost literally. For he referred not only to the independent and international character that transcended the petty politics of the various German states, but above all to its self-sufficiency and "its power to separate the man of letters from other classes in society."[4]

It was a vision of scholarship, not institutional reform, that first lured American students to Germany. And it was the new scholarship, and not primarily institutions, that excited their admiration when they arrived. And it was scholarship that many of them tried to bring back with them.

The German professors and students were immediately impressive, not only for the individual range and depth of their knowledge in the classical languages and literatures, but more for their systematic conception of that knowledge. They appeared to have a historical command of their subject that seemed far beyond the capabilities of even the most advanced and learned college teachers of Ticknor's day.

The German professors also appeared to wear their knowledge differently. Men like Boeckh, Hermann, Wolf, and others did not for the most part use their vast classical learning to embellish belle lettristic essays. They had a different audience and a different purpose for their writings. And they seemed to treat the classical world less like a public park in which anyone is free to wander as he wishes, than like some kind of restricted collective farm, owned and intensively cultivated by a select group of inhabitants. The standards for access to the farm seemed more rigorous than anything that American students from the time of Ticknor to the end of the century thought possible.

The Germans had a firm conception of the role and duties of scholars and scholarship in the humanities, of the criteria of scholarly conviction, and a sense of territory and community in which these operated, that were quite startling to the earliest American students there. At the time when the first Americans came, the criteria and especially the practice of scholarship were by no means universal. Only Göttingen, the new University of Berlin, and to a lesser extent Halle, could be considered homes of the new scholarship. But the ideal was there, expressed not only in the external forms of universities, seminars, growing numbers of students and professors in the humanities, and in the rhetoric surrounding these, but also in the solid works of history and philology beginning to be produced.

The documented history of the external forms, embellished with a few rhetorical flourishes from Humboldt or Fichte, is commonly taken as the history of scholarship. And the University of Berlin is taken not just as "the model of the nineteenth-century German university"[5] but as the sole source and site of the academic revolution which its founding expressed. But the university was neither built in a single day nor out of thin air. Nor did it spring fully armed from William von Humboldt's brow in 1808–10. The university could not have gained acceptance or influence or grown so rapidly if the conception (though not yet the widespread practice) of scholarly teaching and research that was its proclaimed mission had not preceded it.

To twentieth-century Americans the conception of research is deceptively simple. And the histories of education grappling with the problem of what constitutes scholarly research most often enumerate the dates and places of the founding of scholarly journals and philological seminars. But there were philological seminars and scholarly journals long before there was a modern idea of scholarship. And they do not illuminate more subtle problems of what constitutes a scholarly question, how it arises and is recognized as such, what is and what is not scholarly territory, how scholarly questions are to be addressed, and what methods and solutions will suffice to convince that community which presumed to promulgate these invisible laws and criteria.

These are, for the most part, inner laws. And the process of their acquisition is not so much an intellectual as a social and psychological one. There are unspoken metaphors at work here: of frontier, knowledge and its pursuit as limitlessly moving; of quest, the scholar's activity, not as a passive guardian of knowledge, but as its active seeker; of field, the staking out, fencing in, and farming of a portion of the frontier; of settlement, the orderly growth of communities on the frontiers of knowledge; and law, the protection of these communities by recognized and enforced standards. These are some of the more striking internal metaphors of modern academic scholarship in the humanities and the sciences. They have an air of the nineteenth century about them. It is often thought that they emerged first in the sciences, from which the humanities and social sciences drew their examples.

But modern academic scholarship appeared in the humanities long before it had been established in the sciences. And the metaphors which govern scholastic self-awareness were operating within the well-defined disciplines of classical and comparative philology long before any kind of recognizably modern chemistry, physics, geology, or biology was practised in the German universities. In fact, those humanistic disciplines began to emerge in the German universities in the last three decades of the eighteenth century. It is in that convulsive period of German history that we must look for the beginnings of a distinctive academic vocation and ideology.[6] These were partly the result of specific breakthroughs in methodology, particularly in philology. But these breakthroughs, in turn, depended on a whole set of cultural forces which operated in Germany throughout the last few decades of the eighteenth century.

The internal social and psychological rules of a closed social group (which in this case happens to be an intellectual and academic group) are determined by its role, whose definition is often the result of a delicate balance between internal forces (those generated by and operating within the group) and external demands (the conceptions and expectations placed on the group by outside forces). In chapter 2 I will discuss some of the internal forces as they are manifested in rhetoric designed for the scholarly community. But I want first to suggest some of the external intellectual forces which affected the definition of a scholarly role in the period just before American students first came to study at German universities.

Perhaps the major intellectual movement which influenced the development of scholarship in the humanities in this period of German history was *Neuhumanismus.* It is a broad, even vague term, which has been variously defined as both an impulse emanating from classical philology and a general humanistic revival throughout German intellectual life. An inclusive definition of *Neuhumanismus* might see it as the use of the language and literature and other cultural artifacts of past cultures, especially that of Greece, for the development (*Bildung*) of the analytic and creative powers of modern individuals and cultures. The movement is usually defined as having originated in the middle of the eighteenth century as a new literary and historical conception and use of classical languages and literatures by such philologists as J. A. Ernesti, J. M. Gesner, and C. G. Heyne. Broad definitions of *Neuhumanismus,* like that of Friedrich Paulsen,[7] extend the movement to include such diverse figures as Herder, Winckelmann, Voss, Humboldt, and even Goethe, as well as a large number of German classical scholars such as F. A. Wolf.

However narrow the definition of *Neuhumanismus,* it does involve at least three major intellectual forces within the Germany of the last part of the eighteenth century, each of which in its own way contributed both to that movement and to an external definition of the role of scholarship. The three subjects of historicism, the classical (or more accurately the Greek) revival, and educational reform in universities and secondary schools have already filled libraries of historical work. I do not want to attempt an intellectual history of pre-Ticknorian Germany in the following pages. I only wish to suggest briefly some of the more obvious relationships between these three intellectual movements and *Neuhumanismus* which affected scholarship in the humanities.

The search for ethical and aesthetic criteria to counter what were perceived as the prevailing rationalist standards of literary and historical criticism occupied the attention of German thinkers as diverse as Hamann, Herder, and Lessing throughout the 1760s and 1770s.[8] Hamann's mysterious irrationalism and Lessing's urbane balance, though influential, did not ultimately serve as alternative sources of values. But Herder's historicist position was a weapon of unimagined power in combatting what was perceived as the barren cosmopolitan values. The struggle against the French Enlightenment was fought on historical ground.

When Herder wrote that "each nation has its center of happiness within itself, as a sphere its center of gravity,"[9] he was insisting on the integrity and self-sufficiency of every culture—its ideals, values, literature, rules, and methods—against standards which spuriously claimed their universality.[10] A critic, in Herder's view, could not apply or impose the values of his own day to the works of another culture. He had, rather, to enter into the "spirit" of that culture, to understand its particular cultural forms, its characteristic "genius," and its individual contribution to the development of humanity. He had to suffuse himself in the language, literature, art, and history of the culture in order better to grasp its particular indigenous character.

The use of the historicity of culture as a weapon against universalistic aesthetic and ethical criteria thus implied the mastery of enormous amounts of specific and largely historical knowledge and gave the advantage to critics with that kind of detailed command. Herder recognized this himself, with his considerable researches into such subjects as ancient Hebrew and classical literatures and the folk songs of many cultures. His "arguments" are most frequently either an expression of his understanding of the spirit of a culture or a celebration of its specific literary or artistic artifacts. Every time that he persuades his readers to recognize the validity and beauty of any work of art or literature of another culture, he has, in effect, made his point.

Herder's own scholarship was certainly effective and acceptable for his own day. But he had chosen a position which was vulnerable, given his own amateur scholarship. Anyone more versed in the specifics of any of his subjects could easily contradict his assertions. If one's values depend on historical knowledge and understanding, then the advantage in any debate shifts to the person with more of that type of knowledge. Thus, the inescapable property of the historicist position is that it quickly converts aesthetic concerns into historical ones. In any historical argument, the specialist has an insurmountable advantage. The Göttingen Historical School had in Herder's day proved that. The capacity for specialization (by such means as a decentralized and competitive university system)[11] is vital. But the impulse and need for specialization are equally crucial. The historicist ground that Herder helped choose and that the *neuhumanistische* scholars for the most part accepted, supplied one of those impulses.

This tendency toward specialization, however, represented a fundamental contradiction for both Herder and *Neuhumanismus.* Not only did Herder personally not have much use for specialists,[12] but his whole idea of the "spirit" of cultures as primary made literary and historical knowledge more mysterious, uncertain, unconcrete, and difficult for specialists (or anyone else) to apprehend. If a spirit is more elusive and more difficult of apprehension and communication than fact, and if specialists deal in facts, then a contradiction is present. It was resolved before it was noticed by assumptions that were both arbitrary and durable. These were brilliantly and succinctly expressed by Humboldt:

History does not primarily save us by showing us through specific examples, often misleading, what to do and what to avoid. History's true and immeasureable usefulness lies rather in its power to enliven and refine our sense of acting on reality, and this occurs more through the form acting through events than through the events themselves.[13]

This is an extension of the attitude of Heyne, Voss, and others that literature and history work by educating our sensibilities.[14] The assumptions are both that a knowledge of "specific events" leads to a knowledge of forms, and that the task of the scholar is to apprehend and communicate both. A specialist's knowledge is still desirable.

The culture that Herder and Humboldt and the *neuhumanistische* scholars used as the prime example of this historicist position was that of ancient Greece. Herder's writings, along with those of Winckelmann and Lessing and a host of others, had established the image of ancient Greece as the "temple of beauty." According to Herder, and his thoughts on the matter were expressed independently and endlessly by nearly every other writer of the period, "from the works of the Greeks the daemon of humanity speaks clearly and intelligibly to us."[15] *Daemon*, of course, means divinity, and it is a particularly revealing word in this context. Herder invokes a kind of oracular, divine power from the literature of ancient Greece, a power charged with mystical and even dangerous portent. No wonder that Schiller exclaimed with exasperation, "Scarcely had the cold fever of Francomania left us when Graecomania burst out even more heatedly."[16]

The infatuation with the Greeks centered on whatever was perceived and endlessly extolled as the spirit of Greek culture. This spirit could be anything and was more commonly everything that the extoller wished: "true humanity" (F. A. Wolf); "something more than earthly, almost godlike" (Humboldt); "almost all human wisdom" (Voss); "the birth of all literature" (J. A. Ernesti); "beauty and exactness of thought, the noble expression of civility" (J. M. Gesner); "beauty and goodness" (καλοκαγαδία) (Heyne)—to give only a sample of this kind of rhetoric.

All this was supposed to be derived, not from a casual acquaintance with the Greek authors in translation, but from a deep appreciation of the qualities of Greek language, literature, and art. Winckelmann had stimulated the popular appreciation of the latter with his erotic paeans to Greek sculpture and the spirit it expressed. Early *neuhumanistische* scholars like Gesner and Ernesti did the same for the language of Greece:

Great was the fortune of the ancient Greeks in this respect: the language in which all learned cultivation was concluded, they imbibed with their mothers' milk.[17]

The image proved an appealing one, and generations of German thinkers, writers, and educators echoed it and Wolf's statement that Greek was the "Muttersprache der Musen."

This was more than an aesthetic observation. German philologists like Heyne and Wolf used the Greek language as a means to understanding Greek history and culture:

Speech, the first creative act of the human spirit, contains the entire stock of general ideas and forms of our thought which has been achieved and will be constructed by the progressing culture of mankind.[18]

For Wolf and the philologists who followed him this was a methodological as well as an aesthetic dictum. Language became the means by which they could research, not only the authenticity of specific literary texts or manuscripts, but also the values and spirit of each culture studied. To them, the dictum was no mere rhetorical flight; it could be taken quite literally. Homer revealed himself and his culture through his language as much as (and some claimed even more so) than through the content of his poems.

Homer's language had been appreciated long before the advent of these German philologists. Their achievement, however, was to make of this appreciation a path to knowledge. The Greek authors were not to be used merely as models of style and expression or for moral exempla. Rather, Greek literature was to be looked to as a whole to stimulate aesthetic awareness and moral intellectual growth. And this use required a more sophisticated and broader use of the classics. *Neuhumanistische* scholars and educators recognized the achievement of Renaissance humanism in reviving Greek learning and using it for exemplary ends. But they criticized the dull Latinate culture and curriculum which had come down to the eighteenth century for obscuring the beauties and literary excellence of the classics behind years of grinding grammatical drill. They aimed for a broader and more sublime understanding.

The whole subject of the Greek revival in Germany and its central position in Romantic art and thought is too vast for adequate treatment here. I only want to suggest some of the ways in which it reinforced a more positive and active role for scholarship. To do so I want to discuss briefly the way in which the Greek revival was used as a polemical weapon, as a model for social and educational thought, and as a source of a specific ideal of education.

The use of classical models, figures of speech, and political and moral exempla was common throughout the eighteenth century. But the *neuhumanistische* use of antiquity proved far more ambitious (and perhaps less straightforward) than the simple "help towards independence"[19] that Peter Gay sees as the Enlightenment use. There was an involvement which for many amounted almost to a morbid fascination with the Greek world, a fascination which may reveal central anxieties of Germans in the last part of the eighteenth century.[20] To equate these anxieties with a simple, provincial insecurity about social or political impotence or the paramount position of French culture is to put the matter all too bluntly. The feeling of men like the young (or for that matter the old) Humboldt, who railed against the misfortune of having been born in the modern world, appears too personal for that kind of easy social psychology.[21] Whatever their anima and etiologies, these insecurities proved strong enough to compel the use of classical antiquity, not just as a refuge or an occasional polemical aid, but as the principal battleground and weapon in generational and cultural struggles.

The common familiarity of every educated man of the eighteenth century with the classics made them, however, into difficult, if natural weapons. Combined with the resolution to seek out the ineffable spirit as well as the grammar, style, and contents of ancient literature, this choice of weapons required an unusual amount of specific and obscure classical knowledge. The certitudes of centuries of "easy, intimate traffic"[22] with antiquity could only be attacked, breached, and overturned by arguments and evidence of considerable weight; the price of conviction was higher and was to be paid in new skills, techniques, and knowledge. The need for substantial issues and sustained argument could best be satisfied by detailed scholarship.

No sooner had Greece been established as the repository of superior learning and moral virtue than German scholars accepted the task of praising the gods and passing the ammunition. The results were only too quickly apparent. The range and depth, let alone the particular concerns of the scholars, soon put the subject beyond the reach of even well-educated men. Classical allusions did not cease. But it was gradually learned that unless one confined oneself to what had already been "proven" by the scholars (or what was held by them to be trivial or incontrovertible), one had better leave statements about classical antiquity to those who devoted their lives to it. Herder had not only made himself look foolish for his stubborn defense of Ossian, he (among many others) had also undermined his own authority (at least in posterity) by gainsaying the careful conclusions of Wolf with little more than bluster.

Yet the increasing encroachment of the academic world did not destroy and may have enhanced the use of Greece as a model. It became a utopian vision of perfection, and in the blasts of *neuhumanistische* rhetoric a particular type of utopia, a vision of creativity.[23] The earlier partisans of the ancients at the beginning of the eighteenth century had often based their claims on the clarity, elegance, and finished quality of classical thought and literature, and often interpreted the history of classical literature as a progression toward regularity and order. Later partisans such as Winckelmann, not having the same enemies, had no need for the same values, and their interpretation differed. The extreme aesthetic judgments which informed Winckelmann's historical view, his elevation of the Greeks at the expense of the Romans, marked this shift among partisans of the ancients. The new values were simplicity, passion, the use of styles and images to induce sublime feeling, and, above all, creativity. Their "Dämon der Menschheit" was far from being a purely ethical ideal, but, as Cassirer remarks, extended "to every creative act whatever, regardless of the sphere of life within which it realizes itself."[24]

As Greek art and literature became the living model of creativity, so the images and styles of that culture assumed an even greater relevance for a German society obsessed with that ideal. And the values of direct expression, simplicity, sublime emotion, and power which were found in Greek art coincided with the values of the primitive revival. Greece took its place as the supreme primitive among the ancient Hebrews, old Norse, and Anglo-Saxons, among others.[25] German scholarship had both a ready market and a diversity of subjects for elaborating alternative cultural values and forms.

It had to be a scholarship capable of elaborating alternative values and models of this particular sort. J. M. Gesner's and J. A. Ernesti's editing and annotation and the other specialized eighteenth-century indices, compilations, and catalogues were not sufficient for a public (or students) whose appetite had been whetted by the grandiose claims of a Winckelmann. The Grecian and other utopias did not demand any dramatic re-ordering of political or social values, let alone any political action or organization. In fact, they may have been the more appealing for their remoteness and political innocuousness. But the demand was for a particular and sophisticated kind of research and description of these societies which only full-time, long-term commitment could offer.

Even as Italian "antique factories" tooled up to supply the demand for classical ruins and artifacts, so new supplies of scholarship began to meet demands—not that there was ever a sellers' market for disquisitions on a theme of the digamma, though the stuffy results of the learned societies could serve a surprisingly large public. Instead, the principal market for scholarly production in Greek and other utopias proved to be the classroom. It was not men of letters like Diderot or Chateaubriand or social mystics like Fourier who elaborated these utopias, but rather scholars like F. A. Wolf, K. Lachmann, Friedrich Ast, and August Boeckh who embroidered the vision of Greece and merchandised it in durable form: education.

Paideia, the Greek concept of education which Werner Jaeger was much later to consecrate as the central expression of Greek humanism, had assumed this role in German *Neuhumanismus* a century and a half before. Jaeger's description of the relationship between *paideia* and *humanitas* could have served as well to describe the connection between *Bildung* and *Neuhumanismus:*

humanitas meant the process of educating man into his true form, the real and genuine human nature. That is the true Greek paideia. . . .[26]

The four senses of the Greek word—child-rearing, education, mental culture, and the raising of plants or animals—were precisely duplicated by "Bildung." More important, the mystical aura of untrammeled personal development of personal powers and faculties to some kind of transcendental fulfillment which clung to the Greek word adhered even more strongly to the German. *Bildung* became the fervent personal concern of nearly every German writer of the period. As Friedrich Schlegel said: "The highest good and the only useful thing is education."[27]

The concept of *paideia* or *Bildung* could function both as an archetypal theme and as a radical educational countervalue. As an aesthetic image it was transformed by German and other

Romantic writers into the myth of the relationship between self-awareness and the world. The progression of the self through a process of education and increasing awareness—*Wanderschaft*—became a staple of poetry and fiction. But the image was powerful enough to have become a paradigm for educational theory as well. It became a major point of contact between the literary Greek revival and the movement for educational reform in secondary schools and universities.

As Herder and Winckelmann had used the model of Greek creativity as a weapon against constricted rationalist aesthetic values, Heyne, Gesner, Ernesti, and their successors used it as a weapon against constricted educational values and curricula. They fought hard for new approaches to teaching Greek language and literature. Their textbooks and commentaries infused a new spirit into Greek pedagogy. And they made *Bildung* into the code word for creativity, which they elevated into the highest educational value.[28] "The most well-rounded education promotes the surest sense of beauty: [so] that a mind nourished with Greek ideas grasps the necessary knowledge more adaptively and uses it more flexibly and fruitfully," as Voss declared.[29]

This fortuitous permeation of the Greek classics with the ideal creativity was happily exploited by educational reformers of every stripe. There was a congenial confluence of interests between reformers as diverse as Pestalozzi and Heyne and Greek propagators like Winckelmann which armed the reformers with both the indisputable authority of classical models and the fashionable penchant for primitive cultures.

Again, it was a confluence of interests which could only strengthen the role of scholarship. If the aim of *Bildung* was the unhindered growth of the powers of the individual, and if the best means for this was saturation in Greek literature and history until the secret of its creativity revealed itself, then a scholarship that claimed to reveal these things was clearly a legitimate part of education. And *neuhumanistische* scholars did claim this, starting with Heyne, of whom his biographer and son-in-law said quite justly:

His entire vision of antiquity can be called a poetic one. This view, and the treatment of antiquity that grew out of it, must, however, give an entirely new force and direction to the entire field. He viewed it from its most beautiful, but equally from its truest, side. Therefore, this meant that not merely language study but much more the cultivation of taste, the ennobling of sensibility, and the fulfillment of our entire moral nature would be stimulated by this study.[30]

Heyne would probably not have insisted on the separation of the most beautiful and the truest sides of antiquity.

When Heyne and Gesner railed against the dead Latin curriculum of German schools and universities, they spoke with the triple authority of teachers forced to deal with its products, former inmates of the system, and scholars whose researches had convinced them of the existence of an alternative living reality of classical culture. It is difficult to say which role carried the most weight. But when they and their successors advanced this reality, not only as infinitely preferable to dull grammatical incantations, but also as a vital necessity in education for self-awareness and creativity as well as for the advancement of art, literature, and mankind, they were believed. This image of classical life and creativity was based, however, not so much on the actual product of scholarly researches, as on a rhetoric whose commitment to relevance was to prove greater than the capacity of subsequent German scholarship to fulfill it.

The close interrelationship among the movements of historicism, the Greek revival, and educational reform may have become apparent in the preceding pages. All three movements were to some extent polemical. And they appeared to have perceived at least one common enemy: aesthetic and educational values that were thought of as artificial, stifling, uncreative, shallow, and essentially French. All three movements called for more humanistic and sublime values in art, literature, education, and scholarship. Al three movements tended to make much of their case within the terms of a particular knowledge of classical antiquity. They all pressed for a deeper and more extensive study of Greek language, literature, and history. And they all embraced the idea of *Bildung* as central to these concerns. Taken together, these three movements provided a powerful external source and reinforcement of a greater role for scholarship in the humanities. They provided justifications for taking the scholarly approach to knowledge and education. And they furnished opportunities for scholarship to be used polemically in a way that maximized the effectiveness of scholarly thoroughness, vocation, and particular command of historical data. That scholars were in the forefront of all three movements reinforced the new conception of the role of scholarship internally as well as externally.

Historicism, the Greek revival, and educational reform were not, of course, completely separate movements. In fact, they often enlisted the same people within their ranks. And hanging over all three was the dominant intellectual force of German intellectual life: Kant.[31] His influence was so great that it is impossible to measure. Yet, it is important to note that *Neuhumanismus* from the beginning is far more adapted to a Kantian than to a Lockean or Cartesian approach. Historicism, the Greek revival, and educational reform had all insisted on the distinctiveness and internal dynamics of past cultures as a part of their historicity. They pointed to an ineffable noumenal world of past culture and emphasized both the importance and the difficulty of transcending phenomenal remains to penetrate the hidden rationalities of the historical *ding-an-sich.* They were satisfied neither with an empirical nor a dualistic world. And their hunger for the apprehension of the "spirit" of past culture imparts a special humanistic character to German *Neuhumanismus.*

Neuhumanismus, then, is a difficult and complex term. The English equivalents of "new humanism" or "neohumanism" are quite inexact and misleading; there are many groups and individuals who call themselves "new humanists" for quite different reasons. If the German movement is more specific, its definition is not. I have already mentioned Paulsen's generous inclusiveness. Such disparate figures as Gesner, Goethe, Hamann, and Ranke are brought together under that umbrella. An older Brockhaus also has this expansive conception, while a newer edition restricts *Neuhumanismus* to a few classical philologists. I should like to suggest a definition that is somewhere between these and locates it in the interstice of historicism, the Greek revival, and educational reform. Its central core of belief lies precisely in that interstice and includes those things that I have already outlined as belonging to all three movements.

I have discussed some of the loose and implicit connections between *Neuhumanismus* and scholarship. But I have not yet connected *Neuhumanismus* with any particularly modern form of actual scholarship in the humanities. One difficulty of this latter task is the impossibility of gauging the "effects" of any intellectual movement. Was there a change in the German universities in the last decades of the eighteenth century?[32] And was this change at least partly an expression of *Neuhumanismus?* I think so, especially at the universities of Jena, Göttingen, and Halle. But there are few, if any, external signs of this. There was no dramatic increase in student enrollment, faculty chairs, or library volumes in that period. The beginning of this expansion lay a decade or two in the future.[33]

But there was a movement within German scholarship in the last decades of the eighteenth century which can be considered both the practical expression of *Neuhumanismus* and the decisive link between it and the modern form of academic scholarship in the humanities. That movement took place within what was perhaps the first modern academic discipline in the humanities and the forerunner of many other fields, classical studies.[34]

Classical studies in the last decades of the eighteenth century in Germany acquired what its adherents proclaimed as a powerful and systematic methodology—the philological method—as well as a conception of that subject as a defined and systematic field, and not just a collection of great books. Classical philologists began to think of their task as scholars as not being confined to commenting on the classics but expanding knowledge in this field. Heyne, along with most of his contemporaries, had focused his (considerable) philological powers on producing commentaries and editions. But Wolf and his generation adopted a question (i.e. research) centered technique that allowed for a systematic approach. This methodology and conception of field and role were what was new and distinctive about classical studies.

Hajo Holborn has discussed the connection between *Neuhumanismus,* classical studies, and the modern humanities in terms of the humanistic rhetoric of Schiller, Winckelmann, Niebuhr, and Boeckh.[35] But this humanistic rhetoric was not the most important attribute of the actual classical scholarship of the period. The rhetoric connected the developments within classical studies to wider intellectual trends. It gave legitimacy and a context to the results of the new scholarship. But it did not express what was really new about it.

Holborn repeats the claims of *neuhumanistische* philologists that new methods and understanding were:

> but the means of experiencing the totality of human capacities and making them a power again in the building of a new civilization. . . . instead of mere examination of the texts and monuments of the classical age, it [*Neuhumanismus*] called for an understanding of all the manifestations of Greek and Roman life as expressions of the spirit of classical civilizations.[36]

I have already discussed this kind of rhetoric and hinted at the serious discrepancy between it and the reality of *neuhumanistische* scholarship. At the turn of the last century, in the agonized handwringing that accompanied the criticism and attempted reform of the German Gymnasia, a great deal was said about the corruption of the high ideals of Humboldt, Goethe, and *Neuhumanismus* into arid scholasticism. But the test of that proposition is not to compare the rhetoric of the former time with the performance of the latter.

Was *neuhumanistische* scholarship (like Wolf's *Prolegomena* and Ast's *Grundriss*) really "the means of experiencing the totality of human capacities and making them a power again in the building of a new civilization?" A full answer to that question would require a book in itself. But I would like to suggest tentatively that it was no such thing. This is not to say that it did not satisfy some of the demands imposed by its own rhetoric. But there is a certain amount of delusion and self-delusion in classical studies that begins right from its own text-book explanations of its task and methodology.

Philology, and later comparative philology, was supposed to have been the major methodological achievement of *neuhumanistische* scholarship and the fundamental discovery of classical studies. The word *philology* now suggests a rather forbidding and specialized technique of linguistic analysis. Its meaning in the nineteenth century was less specific and technical, if equally forbidding. Rather than denoting a particular method or technique of analysis, it usually referred to a historical attitude toward language and written sources. If that sounds vague, it is.

The definition of *philology* could and did range from the vague
to the mystical among nineteenth-century German philologists.

The standard conception of philology was expressed by
August Boeckh, professor at Berlin and a foremost German
philologist of the nineteenth century. After expounding and
discarding half a dozen definitions or conceptions, Boeckh
would assert in his annual lecture on the subject: "All the
aforementioned concepts of philology, then, with their narrow one-sidedness removed, enter into the true concept of
philology."[37] But even after this momentous announcement,
Boeckh was not ready to come to a definition. He tantalized
with the hint that: "The higher aim of Philology is the historical
reconstruction of the whole of knowledge as well as of its parts,
and the study of the ideas that are stamped into it."[38]

This is still not a definition. Boeckh goes on to discuss the
scope of the philological concept, the relationship between
philosophy and philology, the relationship of both to all other
sciences, whether philology has any sphere of knowledge
peculiar to itself, the necessity of an unrestricted conception
of philology, and so on for several hundred pages. Then Boeckh
plunges into a survey of classical literature and history that has
very little to do with what went before. The reader is left with
the impression that philology has something to do with the
historical analysis of language, but that its metaphysical implications are so incomparably grand that it could not possibly be
described in mere terms like that.

It is clear that Boeckh's learned and eloquent discourses are
not meant to communicate a simple technique or analytical
method but an immense epistemological or even religious conception. And Boeckh was not alone in this conception of his
field. The point of view can be found in other scholars like
Friedrich Ast, a student of F. A. Wolf and a professor at Jena.
Ast begins his *Grundriss der Philologie* with a broad definition
of his subject as "The study of the classical world in its comprehensive artistic and scientific, public and particular life,"[39]
and then progresses to a conception of his field as the reconciliation of the dualistic nature of West and East, philosophy
and religion:

The classical world is indeed the mediator and harmony of the East
and the West, that is, the religious and the philosophical development;[40]

scholarship and poetry in history:

The classical world is indeed the poetry of humanity; its entire essence was fashioned freely and animatedly. The spirit of the modern world is, by contrast, scientific. . . . Therefore, the modern world can only perfect itself through the cultivation of the entire and original essence of humanity, that is, through unity with the ancient world. . . ;[41]

Being and Form in Spirit:

Indeed, through these one-sided methods of treatment, Philology as mere classical antiquarianism would be materialism, or as mere language study, formalism. For the former comprises pure being and the latter pure form, whereas all life and truth are a spiritual unity of being and form. . . . Being and form are the plurality in which Spirit reveals itself, Spirit itself is its unity.[42]

Ast continues in this fashion, exposing the dualism of nature, life, education, and humanity and their reconciliation through the apprehension of the true spirit of ancient Greece. It is not surprising that Ast names Winckelmann, Lessing, and Herder as his heroes or that Boeckh quotes Schelling's idea of the philologist as standing "with the artist and philosopher on the topmost stage of history; or rather, these two pervade the philologist." Boeckh adds approvingly that philology "approaches very near to man's true self, in its spirit at least, if not its full dimension."[43] This is far from a circumscribed vision of scholarship as "todte Gelehrsamkeit" or "mechanische Wissens." The suspicion dawns that these fulsome elaborations are not so much definitions of a field of knowledge or a methodology, as whole secular theologies of redemption (only an approximate translation is possible):

The goal of our education on the whole, according to this, is to become classical. That means that it works so that each individual is educated according to his whole character, which must not be allowed to be extinguished if the whole is not to become an unspiritual and characterless commonality (along with the spirit of the whole, which reflects the national virtue and pure humanity), so that it should live according to its own life at the same time as in a higher harmony and universality, just as in the universe each particular product has its center in itself, bears the principle of its life in its own nature and power, and, at the same time, lives in the center of the endlessly developing whole, whereby it is a harmonious member and emblem of the allness.[44]

To identify this particular promise of redemption as one or another subspecies of German Idealism is perhaps less important than to realize the significance of its application to a field of academic study which is one crucial paradigm of modern scholarship in the humanities.[45] And to call this mere rhetoric—a pitch for metaphysical snakeoil—does not erase the fact that tens of thousands of German students and perhaps thousands of Americans listened and bought.

According to one credible estimate, nearly 1,700 students registered in Boeckh's seminar in classical philology at Berlin alone.[46] To have done so was a matter of status for Americans, of whom perhaps only a few dozen accomplished it. Of course, both German and American students gained a large amount of specific knowledge from Boeckh's lectures. How much of this secular religion of Philology did they acquire and believe? That is one question I shall attempt to answer for the American students in a later chapter.

Early philologists considered themselves the scholarly representatives of *Neuhumanismus.* And they conceived of their work as furthering its goals and ideals. Even the most practical and least visionary among them believed that their methods and researches and analysis of language and the other "objective" forms of past cultures held the keys to the authenticity and creativity of these cultures, and hence the key to authenticity and creativity for all individuals and cultures. Indeed, this belief was so strong that Boeckh had explicitly to deny that philologists held the sole means to these ideals. It appears almost an act of consummate modesty for him to admit that philology might offer only one way among many.[47]

In all this the rhetoric of practical and innovative scholars has been hard to distinguish from that of a Winckelmann, Herder, or Schelling in their role as social visionaries. It has been difficult to perceive what exactly philologists did, how they operated, and how their actual scholarship could have delivered what it promised. Some of them did attempt to offer visions of Greece, Rome, or other cultures.[48] But as Boeckh himself admitted, the Greeks "lived on bread and wine" and not on "poetry and philosophy" and they "were much unhappier than most people believe."[49]

Yet philologists could not have won so many listeners and

even converts for the quest for the *etymos* had they not delivered something which stirred the imaginations of their readers and students. And, in order to grasp something of the power of *neuhumanistische* scholarship and philology, it is necessary to look behind the explicit rhetoric of its practitioners, rhetoric that inspired their listeners and readers but obscured the actual working of their techniques and results.

Early *neuhumanistische* scholars like Gesner, Ernesti, and Heyne had used philological techniques in their specialized researches. They had even made these methods into the cornerstone of their teaching. But it was Heyne's pupil, F. A. Wolf, who first demonstrated in a practical way the power of the historical analysis of language to penetrate the mysteries and incongruities of the remains of the past to reconstruct historical reality. Previous attempts to postulate the outlines or details of an unknown historical situation had been sometimes imaginative and successful. But these attempts were, in the final analysis, perceived as mere speculation. Wolf's use of what he proclaimed a scientific methodology was both successful and convincing. He was revered for having almost "created" knowledge.[50] Despite the distaste of both scholars and the general public for his actual results, he succeeded both in transforming his field of classical studies and in giving a striking example of the power of *neuhumanistische* scholarship, the kind of power that American students of the humanities in German universities recognized. It was the power that, as Ticknor said, separated the German men of letters "from the other classes in society" and made a new "Republic of Letters."

CHAPTER 2

F. A. Wolf freed his profession from the bonds of theology. This action of his, however, was not fully understood for an aggressive, active element such as was manifested by the poet-philosophers of the Renaissance and was not developed. The Freedom obtained benefitted science but not man.

—Friedrich Nietzsche,
Aphorism 42 *We Philologists*

Who builds us such a royal book as this
To honour a chief-poet, folio built,
And writes above, 'The house of Nobody!'
. . . .
Wolf's an atheist;
And if the Iliad fell out, as he says,
By mere fortuitous concourse of old songs,
Conclude as much too for the universe.

—E. B. Browning,
Aurora Leigh

Those were the days in which the familiar type of the German scholar was generated, the man who complained that the public library only allowed him thirteen hours a day to read, the man who spent thirty years on one volume, the man who wrote on Homer in 1806 and who still wrote on Homer in 1870, the man who discovered the 358 passages in which Dictys has imitated Sallust. . . .

—Lord Acton,
"German Historical Schools"

Prolegomena to Modern Scholarship:
F. A. Wolf's Rhetoric of Vocation

The revolution that produced the modern form of academic scholarship in the humanities drew both on prevailing intellectual forces (discussed in the previous chapter) and on a specific methodological breakthrough in classical studies. The climate in which *Neuhumanismus* arose would have been insufficient had it not coincided with a period of momentous creativity within classical scholarship itself.[1] But there is a problem in ascertaining precisely what constituted this methodological revolution. Many specific techniques which the *neuhumanistische* classical scholars used had been developed since the Renaissance. And the institutions in which they worked seemed very little changed years after a new kind of scholarship had developed within them. The changes were relatively rapid; and they were internal as well as external. They involved the criteria by which scholarship in a given field was evaluated. And they involved, or appeared to involve, a new type of scholarly vision.

When the problem of developing a new kind of scholarship in the humanities first began to trouble America in the second quarter of the nineteenth century, classical studies seemed the most inimical subject in the world to the new German ideas. Why should classical studies in Germany have been the matrix of the new scholarly vision? Part of the answer had to do with the Greek revival. The revival focused on a literature that had originated in a profoundly different and unimaginably primitive form of society. The age, complexity, and historicity of the Greek language, and the fact that there were considerable written remains of its ancient state, gave scholars a vast trea-sure-house of material to investigate. They were also furnished with a persistent and difficult problem: the corruption and unreliability of many of their sources and the difficulty of establishing authoritative criteria to discriminate among them. The problem and the possibilities had been furnished to Eusta-thius, the eleventh-century bishop of Salonika. They had been available to Scaliger, the great Dutch classicist, in the sixteenth century. Both of these men rendered unquestionably great service to classical scholarship. But they had not been modern classical scholars. What was the difference?

The usual answer is that it lies in the German-pioneered con-ception of *Wissenschaft,* of systematic and specialized scholar-ship as the primary goal of classical learning. But scholarship is, after all, what both Eustathius and Scaliger had done. More-over, a great deal of their research had been rather specialized. Eustathius had produced detailed and painstaking commen-taries of arcane textual criticism on the Homeric poems. Sca-liger's work was equally esoteric. The differences between their work and modern classical scholarship appear to escape that embracing word *Wissenschaft.*

Partly, the difference lies in the external conditions of scholarly work. Until the eighteenth century, Greek scholars had usually worked in isolation, and they were few in number, toiling without colleagues or facilities. Discoveries were made and communicated slowly. One commentator might spend a lifetime refuting the work of predecessors of decades or even centuries before.

The German university system, at least after the middle of the eighteenth century, provided the means for speeding up the whole process considerably—and crucially, for speed and frequency of discovery are crucial to modern scholarly work. The lower-school curriculum reforms of the middle of the eighteenth century supplied the German universities with a large cadre of students bearing a more sophisticated and thorough knowledge of Greek language (and sometimes litera-ture) than any in Europe. Classical scholars like Heyne could train hundreds of these students in the most advanced philologi-cal techniques over a half-century of instruction. The German university system thus made possible a quantitative jump in the number of well-trained classical scholars familiar with the most advanced level of classical work.

But all this does not explain the singularity of the modern scholarly vision developed by the German *neuhumanistische* philologists; nor does it reveal exactly what their methodological breakthrough was or what it involved. I would like to suggest at least one paradigm of this scholarly vision by examining a specific work of *neuhumanistische* scholarship. I intentionally eschew the hortatory tracts of Fichte or Humboldt, not because their vision is unimportant, but because in those tracts their rhetoric is conscious and unscholarly. I want instead to examine a work whose rhetoric is less self-conscious, and which communicates a conception of scholarship in language and arguments that were, ostensibly at least, quite functional, a book that was both secure enough in its scholarly acceptance, and provocative and influential enough, to itself have had a real historical effect. I do not want merely to assert that the professional scholar replaced the gentleman of letters—that is already quite well known. I do want to suggest how *neuhumanistische* scholarship differed from what had come before, and specifically how its conception of knowledge and scholarship and their purposes differed from works that preceded.

The most famous and influential work of *neuhumanistische* scholarship in the period immediately preceding the arrival of American students in German universities was the *Prolegomena ad Homerum* of Friedrich August Wolf.[2] It is a curious book; and it did not win immediate acceptance by either scholars or the general public. But in the twenty years from 1795 to 1815, when George Ticknor and Edward Everett migrated to Göttingen, it secured an almost universal academic approval. The *Prolegomena,* like many other monographs of the period, was written in Latin (untranslated for more than a century)[3] in a style that is at best complex and often laborious. Despite its relevant, even topical, subject and thesis, Wolf purposely restricted his audience to scholars.[4] Deadly bibliographical discussions command pages of tedious argument, while brilliant hypotheses are tossed off in a line or paragraph. The most erudite and sophisticated arguments and learning coexist with the most shameless boasting and vituperation.

The book is divided into fifty-one sections or small chapters, some of which are not completely coherent or relevant to the greater argument and structure. The announced structure of the book follows the division of the history of the Homeric text into six periods. This first historical volume was then to be followed by a second critical volume. Not only did this latter volume never appear, but the first volume only covered three of the six historical periods. Incomplete as it was, Wolf was content to let the *Prolegomena* stand in that form, and he did not really make a serious attempt to finish it.

Despite these lapses, the *Prolegomena* is a coherent and systematic monograph with a single sustained thesis: that the composition, compilation, and editing of the two Homeric epics was not the work of a single person, but a historical process in which the text fluctuated before reaching the form in which we know it. Wolf does not deny (as Elizabeth Barrett Browning, among many others, would accuse him) that there was such a person as Homer, nor that Homer probably wrote much of what we know as his poems. Wolf does deny that we can accept the texts of the Homeric poems in the same way as those of a modern poet.

This thesis is developed historically in a way which might be summarized as nine closely argued steps: (1) that the poems were composed when the art of writing was either unknown or little practised in Greece; (2) that the process of oral composition and delivery created difficulties in the texts when the poems were later transcribed; (3) that the poems probably did not exist in a unified form but as a collection of smaller poems; (4) that the poems were transmitted orally by Rhapsodists who committed them to memory as a part of training for their profession; (5) that the extemporaneous style of recitation of these Rhapsodists introduced interpolations and anachronisms into the poems; (6) that a written text of the Homeric epics was probably compiled about the time of Pisistratus, the dictator of Athens; (7) that in the process of transcription, a certain unity was imparted to the poems along with still more errors and interpolations; (8) that there was no complete and authoritative text of the poems until the editorial labors of Aristarchus, a second-century B.C. Alexandrian scholar; (9) that the work of Aristarchus and his predecessors at the Alexandrian library introduced still more interpolations and errors into the surviving

Homeric texts. These conclusions form the essential content of the *Prolegomena*.

They are not difficult or abstruse conclusions in themselves, although the arguments for them frequently are. But they generated an immediate and intense disapproval. Some of Wolf's critics simply misread him. For a century afterward he was accused of asserting that there was no such person as Homer or that, if there was, he did not actually write the *Illiad* or the *Odyssey,* when all that Wolf had actually said was that "Homer was not the author of the *unified form* of his poems" (italics mine).[5]

But even the critics who did not make such mistakes were adamantly opposed to Wolf.[6] Villoison, the eminent French scholar who had edited and published the Venetian manuscript on which some of Wolf's conclusions were based, regretted that his work had been used for such purposes. Voss, the distinguished German poet and translator of Homer, also disagreed with him. Heyne, the foremost German classicist of the day, declined to support Wolf. Scarcely a single scholar, German or foreign, agreed with Wolf.

This was in some ways a curious reaction. For the conclusion that provoked the most controversy, the idea of the oral composition and transmission of the Homeric poems, was neither new nor the most original part of the book. That idea had been raised repeatedly by both ancient and modern critics. Robert Wood's assertion of the theory a generation before earned him praise, not opposition. It was the content of the *Prolegomena* which supposedly offended. But there must have been something else as well. Wolf must have touched a sore spot in the affections of both scholars and the general public.

Homer occupied a unique position among poets both ancient and modern. He was, to be sure, the central figure of the highly partisan *Querelle des Anciens et des Modernes.*[7] But this should not obscure the fact that in some ways he was closer to being perceived as a modern vernacular poet rather than as a classical author bound by the school-learned Latinate rules.[8] He was anything but a mere school poet. Even to those fluent in Greek (though the great majority of his readers in the eighteenth century were not),[9] the Homeric epics were more familiar through translations often more contemporary than accurate.

Bentley's comment on Pope's translation—"It is a very pretty poem, Mr. Pope, but you could hardly call it Homer"—was commonly known, and just as commonly ignored. Critics like Thomas Blackwell, who were well aware of Pope's deficiencies and fabrications, were content to use his translation.[10] This use of vernacular translation suggests a relationship with Homer that assigned him both the authority and status of a classical author and the familiarity of a modern poet.

Homer's robust language, the simplicity and directness of his emotions and descriptions had offended a few eighteenth-century critics. But precisely those qualities enhanced his popular and scholarly image as a primitive poet of a freer and more heroic age.[11] Even those critics who exclaimed over the ordered and disciplined artistic perfection of the two poems, celebrated them for rising above mere order and discipline. To Madame Dacier, the learned French translator, the epics were a regulated and symmetrical garden. To Pope they appeared a wilderness of savage beauties.[12] But to both of them, the poetry came from another and more natural world.[13] If Pope put Homer into eighteenth-century dress, it was perhaps to capture the spirit of that simpler time, rather than, as is usually suggested, to banish it.

There was applied to Homer, a century before Carlyle intoned its high Romantic meaning, a doctrine of natural genius, which made him even more than the "Prince of Poets" whom the previous age had celebrated. Critics insisted on Homer's completely unique powers of sublime description and feeling, his "Poetical Fire," as Pope calls it.[14] Comparisons with Ossian, the Hebrew Patriarchs, and modern Bedouin tribes did not detract from his supposed singularity and genius, but created an image of a poet who stood beyond the strictures of mere analysis, the pettifogging precepts of pernicious pedantry.

It was a highly partisan claim at the end of the seventeenth century. Yet it should not be forgotten that by the middle of the eighteenth century these partisans triumphed. In a sense, their triumph was not so much in defending Homer as an "Ancient," but in converting him partly into a "Modern." They created a symbol that unified high and popular (graveyard school) cultures, and spanned Enlightenment and Romanticism.

If it had done nothing else, the *Querelle* succeeded in domesti-cating Homer and Homeric criticism. Partisan and detractor spoke the language of the day, and not a scholarly jargon. The debate brought Homer very much within the circle of educated, though not necessarily learned, discourse. Even scholarly critics celebrated Homer in a language at once accessible and congenial to ordinary eighteenth-century readers.

There was, of course, a more specialized classical scholarship in Germany and Europe that was carried on by a handful of university professors and a slightly larger number of school-masters, ministers, and sometimes librarians. Sandys, Bursian, and others have chronicled its major activities, principally in the eighteenth century, producing more correct editions of the Greek and Latin authors.[15] J. A. Ernesti, a professor at Leipzig, devoted most of his scholarly work to editions of Cicero, Homer, Callimachus, and Aristophanes. Heyne, who taught at Göttingen for nearly fifty years, was perhaps best known for his editions of Virgil, Tibullus, Epictetus, and the *Iliad.* Other scholars produced immensely useful works like bibliographical summaries, indices of classical authors, special-ized catalogues of numismatic and archaeological collections, translations, and school editions.[16]

But all this more specialized activity was by no means a distinctively modern form of scholarship. It did not, for ex-ample, forge a more reliable and consistent methodology. Even at mid-century the simplest facts about the composition of the Homeric epics were in doubt. Many notes, commentaries, and editorial decisions of even learned and famous classical scholars were judged, by the not overexacting standards of the day, to be not merely deficient but arbitrary and capricious.[17] Nor did even vast labors create a conception of classical studies as a systematic field. Lectures and publications were more often dedicated only to the exposition of individual works of litera-ture. There were no real systematic expositions of the subject such as became the standard work of German and other scholars in the following century.

Even though some eighteeenth-century scholarship was re-stricted to use by other scholars, it did not necessarily take the propagandistic labors of a Winckelmann to integrate much of it into ordinary intellectual consciousness. The three-cornered debate among Lessing, Herder, and Professor C. A. Klotz of Halle, on the place of classical allusions in modern poetry is one example of this eighteenth-century intellectual level.[18] The debate was not mere popular wrangling; but neither was it specialized discussion. Herder's other writings on classical literature are on much the same level: often learned but not specialized. Homer and the rest of classical literature were not the property of a scholarly elite. Useful and even scholarly contributions to the understanding of classical literature could be made in ordinary educated language, in nonscholarly forums, to ordinary eighteenth-century readers.

The two most famous and significant works of eighteenth-century Homeric criticism make the point more specifically. Thomas Blackwell's *Enquiry into the Life and Writings of Homer*[19] and Robert Wood's *Essay on the Original Genius and Writings of Homer*[20] have both been proclaimed as examples of systematic and modern Homeric scholarship.[21] They were not. But neither were they mere popularizations. They were prime examples of this eighteenth-century level of scholarship.

Blackwell, a professor of Greek at Edinburgh, wrote anonymously and in an easy style. He was not ashamed to demonstrate a large classical learning. Nor did he hesitate to display his knowledge of obscure commentators and to quote at length in Greek and Latin, sometimes in the former language as well as the latter without benefit of translation. His exposition of the manners and circumstances of the Homeric age was both brilliant and immensely valuable.

Robert Wood, a former undersecretary of state in Pitt's government and one of the few Englishmen of his century to have traveled extensively in the Levant, was a gentleman scholar and a member of the Society of Dilettanti.[22] He was nonetheless a careful and learned classical scholar whose close readings and brilliant surmises earned his work extravagant praise everywhere. Goethe asserted that Wood "made Homer shine his light above us again."[23] Heyne declared the *Essay* a work of nothing less than genius. Even Wolf gave it grudging admiration.

But neither of these brilliant books appears a work of modern scholarship to compare with Wolf. There is no discussion of sources or manuscripts. The enormous problems and discrepancies in the Homeric texts are not even introduced, let alone explained. Differences in authorities are often superficially resolved. Neither Wood nor Blackwell is consistently critical of the standard authorities; nor do they compare their authorities in any systematic way. Despite Blackwell's sophisticated and even visionary treatment of mythology[24] and Wood's brilliant, animated sense of Homeric social history, both accept Homer's descriptions too readily and literally. Moreover, both critics make assertions that have slight basis in the text or commentaries. Blackwell, for example, vehemently proposes Egypt as the source of Homer's education and cosmogony,[25] a theory with very little support and clearly disproved by a fellow Scot, William Jameson, only a few years before.[26]

Both critics introduce the idea of the oral composition of the Homeric epics. Blackwell dismisses it instantly[27] and Wood supports it brilliantly.[28] The manner of their discussion is instructive. Blackwell does not mention the chief prior authorities for the idea, Josephus or Eustathius, and does not explore the conception or its implications. He assumes that Homer's illiteracy would be a poetic defect and a threat to Homer's reputation. Wood, on the other hand, perceived no threat to the poet in this and used the idea to support his concept of the natural genius of the primitive bard communicating the wholesome simplicity and charm of his age. But Wood's discussion, too, is curiously unsystematic. In neither book is there an attempt to sustain a consistent and protracted argument throughout the work.

Blackwell and Wood follow a topical approach and organization which imparts a certain loose structure to their discussions. But that is inadequate to sustain a focused thesis, and the result in both books is frequently general discussion of disparate subjects. There is no sustained and reliable level of scholarship and no systematic exposition of a single theme.

Both books reinforce the image of Homer as natural poet. In Blackwell's words:

NATURE is the surest Rule, and *real Characters* the best ground of Fiction: the Passions of the human Mind, if truly awak'd, and kept up by Objects fitted to them, dictate a Language peculiar to themselves. *Homer* has copied it, and done Justice to Nature. We see her *Image* in his Draught, and receive our own Perceptions of Men and Things reflected back under different Forms.[29]

Wood echoes these words in his conclusion:

I consider it to have been of peculiar advantage to his original genius, that he was not diverted by any hypothesis from a free and impartial examination of things; and that, whatever his plan of instruction, either moral or political, might have been (for to deny that he had any would be highly unreasonable), his choice of characters for that purpose never carried him beyond Nature, and his own experience of life.

   To this unbiassed investigation of the different powers of Nature, and the various springs of action, not as they are fancied in the closet, transcribed from speculative systems, and copied from books; but as they were seen exerted in real life, we owe the most correct history of human passions and affections, that has ever been exhibited under one view. . . .[30]

If Homer appears to be a sentimental amalgam of Locke and Rousseau, that may not be far wrong, and all the more significant. For Wood and Blackwell are the two foremost critics of Homer of the eighteenth century; and if their conception of him is sentimental and conventional, then that tells us something about Homeric scholarship in the eighteenth century.

   But, oddly enough, this is not a point on which Wolf differed appreciably from his predecessors:

So the Homeric epics exhibit, if they would be somewhat carefully examined, an admirable measure of naturalness and highly gifted originality; . . . thus this art dwells unmistakably close to Nature herself, to a certain degree, in that it was created not from a book out of the planned formulas of a learned science, but rather from a natural feeling for a just and charming portrayal.[31]

Wolf knew and reiterated his predecessors' conception of Homer as a primitive poet both ideally endowed and historically situated to communicate the rough drama of the heroic age in sublime poetic description. Wolf also repeats his predecessors' doctrine that Homer cannot be judged by "the cold regulations of a straightlaced, rhetorical science."[32] It is clear that the differences between Wolf and critics like Wood and Blackwell center less on the content of his arguments and his explicit conception of Homer than on his methodology and rhetoric, from which the enormous impact of the *Prolegomena* must have been generated.

The rhetorical differences between Wolf and his precursors are obvious: easy colloquial style versus turgid Latin, and brilliant topical digressions in contrast to niggling obscurities. And the effect of these differences is clear. The rhetoric of Wood and Blackwell reinforced Homer's position within the comfortable and familiar educated discourse of the eighteenth century. Within the bounds of this kind of discussion, the most subversive ideas were accepted, even the notion of Homer's illiteracy, as long as the aim of the enterprise was to integrate critical ideas into the common reader's understanding and enjoyment.

But that was *not* Wolf's premise. His rhetorical stance quite explicitly as well as implicitly separates him from this eighteenth-century position and segregates Homer and Homeric criticism from a mere common reader. He makes the whole enterprise of reading, let alone enjoying or criticizing, Homer appear to be beyond the reach of any but scholars. The *Prolegomena* is a case study, a paradigm of the segregation of knowledge, its appropriation for scholarship, not by a specific scholarly discipline—for those did not exist in any modern sense[33]—but by a scholarly stance. This scholarly stance is communicated by Wolf's obvious and often repeated scorn for nonscholars and their work: "Those who admire in Homer only the charming poet and care too little about his earlier fate [the history of the poems until they were written down] align themselves more with rhetorical than with critical exposition."[34] This is an important caveat within the tradition of eighteenth-century criticism and scholarship. For it not only indicates the limitations of the traditional view of Homer as "nur den anmutigen Dichter," it also undermines the validity of a nonspecialist appreciation of the poet. According to Wolf, only someone who has worried about the early history of the Homeric poems can possess the kind of knowledge about the context of Homeric society and culture essential to a correct understanding of them. This kind of rhetoric for the first time erects a barrier between a lay reader and a specialist and denies to the former the validity of his critical insights and interpretations.

If the effects of Wolf's exclusionary rhetorical stance are clear, its power is less obvious. The source of power appears to lie in the methodology of the *Prolegomena.* It was the methodology which subsequent histories of classical philology single out as the most important and original part of the book.[35] And if conviction and certitude depend on methodology, Wolf's claims for certitude and conviction should reflect the power of his methodology.

To correct and restore the Homeric text to the original purity of its ancient form: that is the announced aim of the *Prolegomena.* From the first sentence Wolf implies that that is the task at hand and that his new scholarly method will supersede the flippancy or pure drudgery of past efforts, establish a new standard of textual criticism, and rescue the Homeric texts

. . . from the mistakes and impurities which, as a result of their long journey through the age of barbarism, have clung to them in great number and in different forms, and to restore them to their ancient and original form.[36]

Wolf's opening makes it appear as if the problem is merely one of textual corruption in the Middle Ages, and not the composition and editing of the two Homeric epics. It seems that the task of the book will be to correct the standard text of Homer, edited by Ernesti from Samule Clarke's edition, which was based on late Byzantine manuscript sources.[37] Wolf assumed the rank inadequacy of this text from the beginning, and was the first scholar to make extensive use of Villoison's newly discovered *Codex Venetus "A,"* an early tenth-century Byzantine miniscule text, as the principal means of restoration.

The methodological claim of the first sentences is repeated in the succeeding chapters. The reader is informed of a plethora of new scholarly aids (*Hilfsmittel*), including indices, translations, editions, and compilations, which apparently ensure success. Derisive comments on past critics and criticism imply that the wealth of new knowledge and sophistication will banish the absurdities and mistakes of the past forever. Wolf seems to proffer new techniques of manuscript evaluation, comparison, and criticism. He does bring to his task an immense and accurate command of the Greek language and literature, as well as the most extensive knowledge of all the scholarly commentators and grammaticians.

These new philological techniques are never systematically explained or laid out, but Wolf does treat the reader to dazzling displays of his erudition. If his whole method were reduced to one sentence it might be: "to bring small discrepancies into a harmonious order."[38] His historical sense for anachronisms and discrepancies is uncanny. He then focuses on these inconsistencies and errors in the text, ruthlessly eliminating explanations and rationalizations for them, using his knowledge of Greek grammar and history to build new explanations, supporting these hypotheses with evidence and argument, always appealing to the "facts of the matter." His use of the mistakes in the texts transmutes error into the very means of the regeneration of the text.

Everywhere Wolf appeals to the force of "necessary historical laws" or "the laws of historical research" to anchor his solutions.[39] These have the aura of natural law such as that of Newton. They give the impression of unvarying efficacy and applicability. Wolf derives his certitude and conviction not from ancient authorities, but from "what established itself with compelling necessity out of wisely grounded principles, and this result progresses from sound judgment with which Nature herself agrees."[40] Wolf's faith in necessary principles, however, was not philosophically but methodologically grounded. These seemingly Newtonian natural laws are in fact historical laws, the necessary evolution of language. Though Wolf does not in the *Prolegomena* specifically enumerate these laws, he makes it clear that it is from this regular historical evolution that he takes his criteria. He asserts that the criteria for accepting one or another authority or manuscript source cannot come only from an understanding of the context of the text.[41] His understanding of the historicity of the language gives him the authoritative criteria both for resolving the errors of the text and for penetrating more deeply its cultural and social matrix. Wolf's understanding of the historicity of language allows him, indeed leads him toward, an understanding of the historicity of the Homeric text.

This is the great methodological breakthrough that makes

possible his rhetorical insistence on the necessary exclusiveness of classical scholarship and its separation from ordinary educated opinion. It is worthwhile to note that the exclusiveness of the scholarly vocation is based on what is perceived to be its grounding in "scientific" research. The concept of research most emphatically does not stem from the natural sciences, however. It comes directly from Wolf's understanding of languages as evolving according to regular and scientifically predictable laws. And, while many of Wolf's specific discoveries have, of course, been superseded, this idea of the regular evolution of linguistic forms has in general been confirmed.

In the Homeric poems Wolf had found the perfect vehicle for his conception of philological research. Not only did the problem of Homeric composition command the imagination and attention of the educated public as never before (or after) but it demanded every bit of Wolf's specialized philological understanding and allowed for extremely fruitful and innovative insights into the poems, as well as into Greek social and cultural history more generally. It was a fortuitous and rare opportunity for the application of specialized techniques to a general problem. And Wolf used his methodology not only to address this one problem, but to secure the entire territory of classical studies for that methodology.

Methodology was in itself, however, not quite enough. Wolf had still to rely on his exclusionary rhetoric to erect a barrier between ordinary reader and scholar. The effect of his language is to shift the focus of attention away from the methodology and onto the vocation of scholar. The subject "belongs" to the scholar: that is the overwhelming subconscious as well as conscious message of the rhetoric and structure of the *Prolegomena.*

Thus Wolf labors mightily in the vineyard of his own credibility. What is sure and reliable (*sicher* and *zuverlässig*), two frequently repeated words, becomes, in terms of the contents as well as the methodology, one of the central problems of the book. Despite repeated appeals to authorities, necessary historical laws, and scholarly aids, credibility and reliability do not appear to flow only from these. Instead the issue and the problem of reliability revolve around the scholar himself, and the assurance and certainty that only he can generate. The locus of expectation shifts to the character and mediating role of the scholar. Methods, laws, and scholarly aids do not exactly operate like natural laws in the physical universe. Methodology in classical philology (and ultimately in the rest of the humanities) becomes inseparable from the working—the vocation—of the scholar. That, then, is the function of the unconscious rhetoric in the *Prolegomena:* it fuses methodology with vocation.

The immediate impact of the *Prolegomena* seemed to derive from its conclusions. But it came, rather, from the power of its arguments applied to a subject that was tolerably important, if not crucial, in the intellectual concerns of the educators but not scholarly public. It was not a mere succès de scandale. For Wolf had made it impossible to return to the genial acrimony of the *Querelle.* The easygoing ways of eighteenth-century Homeric criticism were rendered obsolete at a stroke. Wolf had banished that comfortable realm of discourse whose universal concerns scholars began to plunder for their private empires.

It did not take long for Wolf's contemporaries to realize this fact. Superficial polemicism quickly expended itself in reviews and a few soon-forgotten books. Serious rejoinder could only arm itself with Wolf's weapon, historical philology.

Wolf did and does convince his readers that he was able to see more deeply into the nature and problems of "the Homeric question." Perhaps more important, he convinced his readers that there *was* something called the Homeric question,[42] for it was Wolf who created it. He did not raise the conjecture; but he converted what had been interesting but incidental into something worthy of sustained enquiry and the full labors of committed scholarship. The most important methodological advance of the *Prolegomena* was this framing of the Homeric question. It became the basis for much of the work of classical scholarship throughout the nineteenth century. More important, it provided a paradigm of the primary attribute of scholarly vision: the power to frame questions susceptible of scholarly enquiry (though not necessarily solution or provability) and of no other kind of intellectual approach.

It was this power which marks a primary distinction between the *Prolegomena* and the work of such predecessors as Blackwell and Wood. They did not lack a large measure of knowledge, sophistication, scholarship, and even specialization. But they did not frame their enquiries in the exclusive manner of Wolf. It was not arguments or knowledge that they lacked, but a specific and exclusionary concept of what a scholarly question was. Without that they could not communicate anything like the vision of commitment, preparation, and concentrated and systematic knowledge of a scholarly field which presupposes a life dedicated to work in that field.

That last word introduces a second crucial distinction between gentlemen like Blackwell and Wood and scholars like Wolf: namely, the latter's conception of his subject as a "field" and his use of that metaphor. It is a complex and difficult metaphor. Loose mention of things like "the field of scholarship" are neither specific nor particularly modern. But Wolf does use the word *field* (*Feld*) and the metaphor in its more restricted, modern sense of a defined area of knowledge which is both limited in its scope (a particular "discipline") and infinitely expanding (through increase in knowledge), both specific to any single scholar's endeavors—"my current field of research," for example,—and a commonly delineated sphere of learning like Modern European Intellectual History.

Wolf certainly demonstrates an acute sense of his work belonging to a defined, specific "field" of classical studies. The German translation of that expression in the *Prolegomena, "der Gebiete der Altertumswissenschaft,"*[43] too freely renders the Latin, *"partium antiquitas."* But Wolf in any case practically invented the German word *Altertumswissenschaft* and was certainly the first to begin to give a systematic exposition of it twelve years after the publication of the *Prolegomena,* in his *Museum des Altertumswissenschaft.*[44]

Wolf also expresses the sense of the scholarly field as being open-ended, subject to incessant change and improvement. He treats the Homeric question as unsolved and perhaps unsolvable in any fixed sense, yet worthy of continuous attempts to solve it: a quest whose goal is both fixed and unattainable. Wolf's own arguments depend on an open-ended dialectical relationship between object and question. He implies often that the object or field determines the questions. But he also speaks of the "field of the question" (*Feld der Streitfrage/campus disputandi*).[45] His particular use of the metaphor of field, both in its general and personal sense, carries with it a conception of self-limitation by means of the question, a "circumference of vision" that is the price of knowledge. This is a limit unknown to Wood or Blackwell.

The metaphor of field does not merely imply a static limit, however. It is the metaphorical, the inner means of appropriating and possessing knowledge, the symbolic vehicle of a scholarly territorial imperative. When Wolf uses an expression like "the field of Homer,"[46] he encloses his subject in a manner which is both peculiar to and necessary for modern scholarship. His vision of Homer as a field, as a context in which specifically scholarly study can take place, is a mechanism of enclosure that again distinguishes Wolf from his predecessors. It is a metaphor which supports both the modern concept of systematic scholarly research in a field or discipline, and a particularly modern idea of teaching, the systematic communication of the results and methods of those research endeavors. The metaphor is founded on inner conviction, and permits a degree of imprecision in the definition of what is and what is not a field in the humanities. This partly allows for a plethora of disciplines founded less on demonstrable distinctions of methodology and subject matter and more on the consensus of their adherents. "Field" is a metaphor that is conducive to the "adaptive radiation," the rapid splitting-off of the subspecies of academic disciplines and their expansion into new ecological niches.

The ephemeral and specifically "inner" quality of the scholarly enterprise is conceded by Wolf in a curious and significant passage in the *Prolegomena:*

We must therefore give up the hope that it would be possible to restore the form of the Homeric poem as it originally was in any other way than in our minds and, at the best, in an unclear outline.[47]

The worth and validity of the scholarly enterprise are assumed at the same time that its ostensible aim is announced as impossible in any but a putative way. The suggestion is that this nearly fictional end is a worthy result of all that scholarly effort. Restoration is only possible in the mind. Thus the scholar, through his work, gives a form to the work of the poet that is at least as valid as any surviving text. The work of the scholar is, in a sense, equated with that of the poet. It is a curious and perhaps irrelevant claim, and it may be limited only to this particular problem, the Homeric question. But it should not be forgotten that the Homeric question was perhaps the original problem of modern scholarship in the humanities.

Three years before Wolf's death in 1824, and eleven before his own, Goethe wrote a small ditty, *Homer Wider Homer,* on the extravagant claims of contemporary Homeric scholarship:

Homer Against Homer

How cleverly have you (like yourself indeed)
Us from veneration freed,
So that we know—a wholesome quirk!
The Iliad's just a potboil work.

But don't anyone feel low,
Since youth knows to ignite us so
That we think it lovelier as a whole
And feel it joyfully as a whole.

Nietzsche seized on this poem as evidence of Goethe's dislike of scholars in general and Wolf in particular.[48] But Goethe, despite periodic blasts, numbered many philologists and other scholars among his friends. And Goethe counted Wolf as one of his good friends for almost three decades, a considerable accomplishment if one remembers Wolf's disturbing tendency to disagree with his friends and vilify those who disagreed with him.[49] At times Goethe appeared dazzled by his friend's brilliance. There is even a report of the venerable genius hiding behind a curtain at Halle to hear Wolf lecture to his students.

Yet, throughout their friendship Goethe harbored substantial reservations about Wolf's work and its effects. According to his diary, Goethe spent the month of April 1797 deeply immersed in Homer and the *Prolegomena.*[50] He spoke favorably of it in public and in his communications with its author.[51] But in a letter to Schiller, he confided a doubt about the work that was to worry him periodically for the rest of his life.[52] He thought the *Prolegomena* not only subversive of the artistic unity of the Homeric epics (an artistic unity essential and central to every work of art), but also dangerous in its objectification of Homer and his poetry.[53] He did not care so much that Wolf saw the *Iliad* as a "potboiler" (*Flickwerk*), but that in freeing the modern world from Homer, Wolf had also rid it of him.[54] He renounced Wolf's conclusions, not so much because he was not convinced but because he fought hard against being convinced. Again and again he returned to the problem, and each time there is a note of plaintive anger in his comments on Wolf and his work.

One of Wolf's friends, however, did not harbor any such doubts, the future minister of culture, religion, and education in Prussia, William von Humboldt. He held his mentor in something approaching awe, an emotion he demonstrated convincingly as soon as he had the opportunity, by working to have Wolf appointed to one of the first professorships in the university which expressed Humboldt's and the modern ideal of scholarship, the University of Berlin.[55] Humboldt did not entirely succeed.[56] But he did help to enshrine Wolf as the epitome of the modern scholar in the humanities.

When he was first matriculated at Göttingen in 1777, Wolf provoked a small but significant altercation with his future teacher, Heyne. Wolf refused to register in the faculties of law or theology, despite Heyne's insistence that there was no other way to use classical learning. The young man persisted in calling himself a philologist, a profession that Heyne told him did not exist. By the end of Wolf's life it did exist.

Göttingen had had a philological seminar for decades. And Heyne had sent forth from it students who were superbly grounded in classical knowledge. But it was the next generation that marked the decisive turn to professional philological scholarship. Among the foremost of the new professional philologists were two students of Wolf's seminar at Halle: Friedrich Ast and August Boeckh. They were a part of the first generation of truly modern professional scholarship in the humanities.

Wolf's last years at Berlin were not productive ones. He had already done his work. His systematic exposition of classical philology in the *Museum des Altertumswissenschaft* and in three decades of teaching and publication helped make it into the model of a modern academic field.[57] But Wolf was best remembered for his *Prolegomena ad Homerum.* He had made it into a paradigm of modern academic scholarship in the humanities. As an expression of *Neuhumanismus* it was contradictory work. It did not fulfill any of the promises of *neu-*

humanistische rhetoric. It did help to destroy the Homer who had existed in the world of ordinary educated discourse and made a new place for the poet as a subject or "field" of scholarly investigation. The *Prolegomena* thereby epitomized the process of scholarship's appropriation of "territories" for its own aims and methods. This was the "aberration" and "atheism" against which Thomas Allen and Elizabeth Browning raved, but to which Humboldt and his successors were blind. It was this which helped to create the new "Republic of Letters" that Ticknor and his successors found waiting for them.

CHAPTER 3

Whene'er with haggard eyes I view
This dungeon that I'm rotting in,
I think of my companions true
Who studied with me at the U—
        University of Göttingen
        University of Göttingen

—Nineteenth-century Harvard Song

Innocents Abroad: American Students
in German Universities, 1815–1870

The problem of determining how much the scholarly ethos of Wolf and German classical philology was transmitted is not an easy one. Even the most eagerly Germanophilic of the returning American students could not resurrect German institutions and values on the other side of the Atlantic. Not only was there considerable resistance to educational reform in America, but there was even more suspicion of reform that appeared to be based only on foreign models, no matter how perfect those models were claimed to be.[1]

Very few of the returning students up to 1870 claimed perfection for German institutions and values. Virtually every one of them realized that American institutions had to grow out of American values. Thus, any historical account that explains the development of American universities purely in terms of German "influence" must be highly suspect. The American universities were not constructed from blueprints shipped over on the Hamburg Line. And American scholars were anything but imitations of their German teachers.

Yet, the fact is that American universities were conceived and staffed largely by people who had studied in Germany. There is no doubt that the German "influence" was transmitted chiefly through the experiences of these Americans. For all the historical speculation on German "influence," however, little factual knowledge is available on this American migration, especially up to 1870. Though it is estimated that between nine and ten thousand Americans studied in Germany from 1815 to 1914, there is not yet an accurate estimate of the numbers before 1870, when the most influential American educators studied there.

Apart from a handful of the real celebrities among the pilgrims before 1870—Ticknor, Everett, Bancroft, and Cogswell in the first group and Daniel Coit Gilman and Andrew White later—it is the migrants of the 1870s and 1880s that have attracted the attention of historians. This attention is due partly to the fact that the numbers in these later decades are many times those of the earlier period. Despite the indisputable fact that virtually every one of the men who built the emerging American universities of the 1870s and 1880s and many of the teachers who staffed them had studied in Germany before 1870, most mentions of the German experience refer only to the later period.[2] Others mention the earlier students in a loose way that assumes that the conditions, situations, and experiences of study in Germany were essentially uniform throughout the century. Herbst refers, for example, to the "ill repute in America of the higher criticism, which flourished among German biblical scholars of the time" without distinguishing in any way to what time (and what group) he is referring.[3] American attitudes toward German biblical scholarship varied considerably from group to group and changed perceptibly over the course of the century.

The image of American students in Germany is of their pursuing specialized professional studies.[4] This may be true for the last ten decades of the nineteenth century, but as will be suggested in later chapters, earlier students may have sought more undefined goals. There is no proof for the statement that "before 1870 most of the American students in Germany had been drawn there by the desire for professional training in the natural sciences."[5] The exact reverse may be closer to the truth. The absence of corroborating evidence points to a glaring need for more careful answers to the most rudimentary questions about the whole group of American students in Germany before 1870. Only after we have answered with some assurance and accuracy such simple questions as who they were, where they came from, what and where they studied in Germany and when, and what they did when they came back, can we begin to inquire after their experiences and values.

It has not been possible to research every one of this group

of American students. But I have managed to assemble a comparatively large sample of the group, which, if it is far from
perfectly representative or accurate, may be highly indicative
of the constitution, values, and experience of the whole. Included in the sample is perhaps the largest single group of
Americans of the first seven decades of the century with advanced training in and knowledge of the humanities and natural
sciences. No fewer than nineteen future college and university
presidents are on the list, many of them noted educational
innovators. Most important, the sample includes a significant
proportion of the total membership of the newly emerging
profession of university teaching, as well as a large group of the
nineteenth-century American scientists.

Useful and indicative as the sample is, however, we must be
sensitive to its biases. The most serious distorion, and one for
which there is no ready compensation, is toward those individuals who later achieved some degree of prominence or who
graduated from the three dozen best-known colleges. Although
there are certainly more than a few representatives of the
obscure, they are, for obvious reasons, less prevalent in the
sample than they must have been in the group as a whole.
This distortion persists in such other of the findings as geographical distribution (the Northeast may be somewhat over-
represented, and the South and West less favored), college
origin (the colleges with the most complete and accessible
alumni records, and particularly Harvard and Yale, are over-
stressed), and subsequent occupation (farming, small business,
and small-town professions may not receive their due).

The more obvious, though perhaps less serious bias, however,
is not the result of lack of information but the reverse. Through
the zealous efforts of a latter-day graduate of Göttingen, we
have a record of nearly all the names of American students who
attended there.[6] Though we could only include less than half
of these names in the sample, naturally the proportion of
Göttingen students is somewhat inflated. This also skews some
of our other information, notably that on the dates of study in
Germany (since Göttingen was more popular in some periods
than in others), and on the subjects which the Americans
studied. A certain amount of commonsense "dead reckoning"
may be all that is possible to navigate more surely and counter

this bias of the data. Even with these biases, however, the sample may be of some use in obtaining a rudimentary knowledge of the whole group of Americans who studied in German universities before 1870.

Our first problem is to determine with as much accuracy as possible the size of the group with which we are concerned, for the existing estimates are little more than rank speculations. Shumway's list of American Göttingen graduates, including auditors and nonmatriculates, lists a total of 261 names up to 1870. He compiled his list primarily from the university records, supplemented by the record of the Colony Book, kept by the American students themselves. Given the obligation of aliens to report to the local police and furnish an official reason for an extended stay, it seems unlikely that these records would fail to record many Americans, since the university was perhaps the only reason to stay for any length of time in Göttingen. For the same reason, we have no need to suspect that the Göttingen names are inflated (as the Berlin records might be) with Americans who stayed in the town for other reasons but registered at the university only to be able to claim that they had attended it.[7]

Burke Hinsdale's list of American students at the four universities of Göttingen, Berlin, Halle, and Leipzig up to about 1850 puts the first two universities about equal in numbers.[8] From contemporary accounts of American students of the 1850s and early 1860s, notably that of James Hart, it seems fairly safe to assume that this relative equality persisted at least until the end of the Civil War.[9] After that the indications are that an increasingly larger number of American students made the Prussian capital their destination. Still, in the interval of five years between the end of the war and the close of the period with which we are concerned, this difference could not be very great, and the relative proportions should be quite close. The total at Berlin is probably no less than the 261 recorded for Göttingen and is likely to be slightly more, perhaps as much as 300. If the same proportion holds, the forty names from Heidelberg would indicate 120 for that university. Checks of incomplete registration records at Heidelberg show that this could be somewhat low.[10] Until the 1850s, Heidelberg was somewhat neglected by Americans, although as many as two or three dozen American students could have registered there before 1850. After that date, however, the university gained favor rather rapidly. Justin Winsor's letters from Harvard indicate that he knew three or four other Americans during the time he was there in 1853. By the middle of the 1860s, James Morgan Hart records seeing eighteen or twenty of his countrymen idling the afternoon away in a streetside cafe. He thought that this might have represented about half of the Americans there.[11] But the records do not indicate anything like that number actually registered.[12] Moreover, Hart's observations apply only to the summertime, and he specifically mentions that most of the Americans spent their winters in other universities, so the net registration is particularly difficult to calculate. The rough figure of 120 could not be too greatly wrong up to 1870.

Because the situation at Halle was the exact reverse of that at Heidelberg, with the largest registration of American students in the earlier rather than the later decades, and because of the added check of the Hinsdale list for this time, we can estimate the numbers at Halle with a great deal more confidence. The total of twenty-five names in our sample would, by my rough estimate, yield an actual registration total for Halle of seventy-five. But this seems excessively high. If only eighteen Americans studied there before 1850, and that constituted the bulk of registrations, a total of fifty registrations would be the highest credible.

We must proceed with somewhat less confidence with the figures for all of the other universities combined. Here, because of the large number of institutions and the consequent greater possibility of variation, we might be safer to stick to the rough estimate of 180. This brings us to a total of 910 if we accept the scaling for Heidelberg and Halle. This figure of 910 represents a total of registrations at the universities rather than the actual number of American students. Since a great many of the Americans followed the normal German practice of studying at more than one university, we shall have to scale down the first total to arrive at the desired number.[13] If we scale down this hypothetical total in the same way as our sample, we should reduce it by about 30 percent (343/264), which gives us a figure of approximately 640. Thus, our sample probably includes between a half and a third of the whole group of Americans studying in German universities before 1870.

This figure of 640 (plus or minus at least 15 percent) contrasts sharply with the figure of 1,500 which Charles Thwing gives and the extrapolations of those figures offered by Richard Barnes.[14] The latter's total of 2,200 seems rather excessive. Thwing's calculations, too, appear quite high. However, if we accept his number, we must reduce his total by 30 percent to make allowance for multiple registrations, which he does not. But even with that calculation, Thwing's estimate requires us to believe that there were hundreds of American students at one time studying in Berlin at the end of the 1860s, a situation which is quite improbable for that time and which no observer indicates until the 1880s.[15]

A glance at the figures for university registrations will confirm some of the points we have been discussing. The total number of registrations throughout the whole decade of the 1860s at Berlin was 31. Now, our figures for Berlin are admittedly low. But the equivalent number for Göttingen—for which we have virtually every registrant—is only 45.[16]

Taking the figures more systematically, decade by decade, will yield further insights. Out of a total of 55 registrations (some students registered in more than one university) in the period between 1810 and 1840, Göttingen has 25 (or 45%) and Berlin 16 (29%). Halle, Heidelberg, and all the other German universities share the remaining 13 students (25%) among them. With three-quarters of the registrations of American students in these first three decades, the predominance of Göttingen and Berlin is quite marked. This disproportion may be slightly aggravated by the distortions of the sample discussed above. But the preponderance is something that is readily confirmed by the direct reports of the American students themselves.[17]

We shall discuss some of the reasons for this early lead below. Partly it was due to favorable reports that came back from the first American students there. Despite substantial gains in numbers at Heidelberg and the other universities in the 1850s and 1860s, this lead was maintained until after the Civil War. Even in a sample in which they are underrepresented, Heidelberg registrations go from 1 out of 55 (2%) in the period 1810 to 1840, to 22 out of 127 (17%) in the 1860s. Halle, by contrast, from 7 out of 55 (13%) in the first period and 11 out of 60 (18%) in the 1840s, drops to 3 out of 127 (2%) in the 1860s. The other universities—principally Bonn, Leipzig, and Tübingen—go from 6 registrations (11%) to 26 (20%), although this rise is also underrepresented.

The very sharp drop in registrations at Göttingen in the 1840s, from 25 out of 55 (45%) to 7 out of 60 (12%), is in direct contrast to the increases at the other universities, in all of which the total for that one decade exceeded the total for the previous three decades. Göttingen quickly recovered its American students, however, and despite this temporary drop retained its relative equality with Berlin.

It is clear that the 1840s marked the first of about three quantum jumps of registrations of Americans in German universities. The rate of increase is sustained throughout the 1850s to the Civil War. Although the absolute numbers of Americans did not decline through the Civil War, the rate of increase slowed down until the second of the great quantum jumps at the end of the 1860s and beginning of the 1870s.

These changes in patterns of enrollment throughout the first seven decades of the century are accompanied by changes in the patterns of study in the German universities. Throughout the entire period the philosophical faculty, which includes both the humanities and the natural and social sciences, is dominant, enrolling 158 out of 264 American students. This is by no means due to the preponderance of the sciences in this period, however, as Herbst asserts, for the marked growth in those disciplines does not occur until the very end of the period. Only 4 out of 24 students in the years before 1840 registered to study the sciences. This rose to 8 out of 18 in the 1840s; 23 out of 54 in the 1850s, and 34 out of 54 in the 1860s.

Another very palpable trend is the rapid decline in the numbers and proportion of American students registering in the Theological Faculty after 1850. From a high point in the immediately preceding decade, when 14 out of 47 American students went to Germany to study theology, registration drops to 8 out of 81, less than 10 percent. This trend parallels the decline in German students in the theological faculty, a development which both Paulsen and Conrad note and attempt to explain. Whether their analysis holds true for the American students cannot easily be determined.[18]

The decline in the American enrollment in the theological faculty is more than compensated for by the growth in law and medicine in the 1850s and 1860s. From 3 of 47 registrations in the 1840s, enrollments of Americans in the medical faculty rose to 17 out of 95 in the 1860s. The great emphasis on clinical observation and surgery which had made the great teaching hospitals of London and Paris the centers of medical knowledge, progress, and education began to be supplemented in midcentury by knowledge derived from the physical and biological sciences, whose natural home increasingly became the new laboratory-equipped universities.

The dramatic increase in the number of law students from the 1840s to the 1850s was largely, though not completely, due to the registration of southerners seeking an alternative to the natural law philosophy and common law tradition endemic in legal education in England and America. Training in the German universities was very heavily weighted toward Roman law and a particularly thorough explication of Justinian. German legal philosophy thus provided an easy base for an attack on the natural rights basis of the abolitionist position. And the fact that Roman law itself had perforce to recognize and make secure the legal position of slavery within the empire is another more direct reason for southern interest in German legal education. With the development of the new American case-method of legal training, along with the abolition of slavery, American enrollment in the law faculties of German universities began to decline in the 1860s.

These trends in faculty enrollments tended also to influence the popularity of various German universities for Americans, since some universities favored one or another study. Göttingen and Berlin remained well-rounded throughout the whole period, drawing proportional numbers of Americans in all four faculties. There are, however, some small but interesting variations even in these two institutions. Göttingen has rather a larger proportion of law students (17 out of 33) than any of the others and a slightly smaller proportion of theological students (15 out of 61). This may possibly be due to Göttingen's general decline in the period when theology was strongest and her resurgence precisely when law enjoyed its greatest popularity. But the relative strength of the latter and the weakness of the former may have more than a little to do with that general decline and resurgence.

Göttingen's great strength in science throughout the first seven decades of the century compared with the relative weakness at Berlin is also noticeable. Forty-one of the 97 scientists in the sample studied at Göttingen, compared with only 18 at Berlin. The latter university showed its strength among American registrants in the humanities, however, enrolling 45 out of the total of 122 registered there up until 1870. Halle registered practically nothing but theologians in six decades, 23 of 25 Americans there in the first six decades until 1870 enrolling in theology. Only two opted for the humanities, while another two registered in both the philosophical and theological faculties. The dominance of the philosophical faculty in the other universities is quite pronounced, however. Seventy-five of the 101 Americans who registered in German universities other than Berlin, Göttingen, and Halle found a home in the philosophical faculty; and these were almost evenly divided between the sciences and the humanities (38 to 37 respectively). In part this overwhelming preference may be related to the fact that these universities did not register a substantial number of Americans until the end of the period. The period of their prominence among Americans thus coincides with the dominance of the philosophical faculty generally in the German universities. Although scientists would make up an increasing proportion of American students in the 1870s and 1880s, in this first period the humanities had a comfortable lead.

One of the problems of counting the registrations of Americans in German universities, however, is student mobility among those institutions. Relatively few of the Americans registered in more than one faculty, and these small numbers do not affect the totals significantly. But at least 88 students out of the total of 264 enrolled in more than one German university, some at as many as three or four. Because so many of the names in the sample were taken from Daniel Shumway's list of Americans at Göttingen, it is not surprising that 40 of those 88 mobile students registered there. But Göttingen's American students do not appear to have been more mobile than those enrolling elsewhere. Eighty-one of the 121 registered only there. A much larger proportion of the Berlin students (47 out of 96) migrated to other centers of learning. Moreover, the number of students who shared these two universities, although high (23), is much less than both the numbers of registrations of Berlin students (47) who studied at other provincial universities and the enrollments of Göttingen students who went to other places than Berlin. The lack of any common students between Halle and Heidelberg does not indicate any lack of mobility among the Americans they attracted but simply confirms that they shared neither a subject nor a period. The greatest proportion of mobile students are those at the provincial universities; only 44 out of 126 of these students stayed in one place. The obvious explanation, apart from the distortion of the sample, is that the American students might first come to the better-known of the German universities and, once settled there, could learn of the reputation of others, to which they could then go. For extracurricular reasons, as well, the Americans might wish to divide their time between the metropolis and the provinces. William Dwight Whitney, one of the most serious of the Americans, found it convenient to spend the winter concert season in Berlin with one Sanskrit professor and the summers in cooler, bucolic Tübingen with another. Many other Americans migrated to Heidelberg in the summertime.

Some of the patterns of mobility among the American students changed in the decades up to 1870. Aside from the Göttingen-Berlin connection, the greatest movement in the period before 1840 is between Halle and Berlin and Göttingen. Interestingly, this traffic diminishes perceptibly exactly when Halle is strongest, in the 1840s. Were the American students of theology in this decade content to find one master and stay with him? Or had the opposing schools of biblical criticism hardened to the point that students could not move as freely among them as they had once done? The numbers and sources are too small to venture an answer now. By the 1850s, at any rate, the movement had virtually ceased for the reason given above, namely the decline of Halle and theological study.

The exact reverse is true for Heidelberg and the other provincial universities, as well as Berlin. A large proportion of the mobile students before 1850 (14 out of 32) were in theology.

After that date the other faculties dominate, particularly the philosophical, which in the 1860s has 22 of the 34 mobile American students. Until that decade most (21 out of 35) of the mobile students in that faculty were humanists. But that situation is reversed in the 1860s, when 16 out of 22 American students in the philosophical faculty studied science at more than one German university. The next largest figure for that decade is in the medical faculty, with seven students. The pattern of mobility indicates that those who registered at more than one university in Germany might have been the more serious Americans, for they include the students of theology in the twenties, thirties, and forties, the humanists of those decades and the fifties, and the scientists and medical students of the sixties.

With these observations on the mobile students in mind, it will be easier to examine the registration in the faculties and universities decade by decade. In the period before 1840 the humanities clearly dominate for all universities but Halle. Berlin had been intended by Humboldt to be the great home of the humanities, but it is clearly Göttingen that exercised the greatest appeal for Americans. Fourteen of fifteen Americans enrolled in the philosophical faculty were interested in the humanities. Göttingen's appeal was not quite as lopsided as that figure might suggest, however; seven Americans studied theology there, while law and medicine each claimed three Yankees. Three Americans studied in more than one faculty. At Berlin the appeal was equally divided between the humanities and theology (7 in each), with only one American for each of the other faculties and two who studied in more than one. Almost all the Americans who registered in two faculties in this period studied theology and the humanities, as did most of the mobile students.

In the decade of the 1840s the general pattern did not change greatly, with the exception of the stunning decline of Göttingen. This evidently was not the result of the decline of interest in any one subject—which explains Halle's drop in the fifties—for all of Göttingen's faculties were affected. One ready explanation for this is the effects of the expulsion of the "Göttingen Seven," which halved the total student population there. In 1837, the centennial of the university's founding, the opposition of seven of the most distinguished members of the faculty (including the brothers Grimm) to unconstitutional decrees of the new king led to the professors' dismissal and a landmark battle for academic freedom. It was not for a decade and a half afterward that registrations there reached the levels of the late 1820s. The resulting loss of Göttingen's prestige appears to have depressed American registration there as well.

By the 1850s, however, Göttingen appears to have recovered its American students in all faculties. The numbers for law are up, and the humanities and medicine are restored. But the greatest increase comes in those studying sciences there, more than all the other universities combined (16 compared to 14). Halle and theology have waned by the 1850s. Berlin has held steady, with only minor decreases. Apart from Göttingen, the great increases are at Heidelberg and the other provincial universities, in the humanities and the sciences.

These patterns among the American enrollments continue to hold throughout the sixties. Göttingen retains its students in all areas, although the proportion in the philosophical faculty has shifted decisively in favor of the sciences, registering 22 of 29 students. Berlin has regained its small losses of the fifties. In contrast to previous decades, however, its students in the faculty of philosophy are now almost evenly split between the sciences and the humanities, 10 and 8 respectively. Heidelberg and the other provincial universities, with the exception of Halle which has not regained its American following, give evidence of the same increase in the sciences, 23 of 33 Americans. Even at this date, few American colleges included much science in their curricula, and there were only a handful of scientific shools. The German universities were not competing for American students, since in any case a B.A. or its equivalent was the normal requirement for matriculation in Germany.

Having examined the patterns of registration and migration of American students from 1810 to 1870 in Germany, we may now turn to questions of their origin and education. The dominant role played by just two colleges, Harvard and Yale, in sending American students to Germany is readily apparent. Of the 228 Americans whose colleges could be traced, 125, or 55 percent, studied originally in those two colleges. Harvard, with 38 percent (15 of 39) of the enrollment in the first three decades and 28 percent (11 of 39) in the 1840s, is clearly predominant in these early decades. Yale's contribution rises from 10 percent (4 of 39) in the period before 1840 to 22 percent (14 of 65) in the 1850s. By the next decade it overtook Harvard, sending 29 out of 84 students (32%) compared to Harvard's 22 (26%).

The journey to a German university approached the proportions of a fad among Yale and Harvard classes after the Civil War. But since most of these students persisted for more than one semester, they cannot be dismissed as mere dilettantes. The proportion of students from other New England colleges holds steady at about 23 percent in the decades up to 1860 and drops to 13 percent (from 15 to 11 in absolute numbers) in the final decade of our period. Throughout the whole period, New York and the other Middle Atlantic colleges contributed fewer students than New England, 40 (17.5%) versus 46 (20%) of 228. Of these students, 25 of 40 came from New York, mostly in the 1860s.[19] The numbers from Southern, Midwestern, and Western colleges are nearly negligible, reflecting somewhat the bias of the sample, although the actual figures from colleges of the latter two regions could not have been too much higher in this period.

Both Harvard and Yale sent students to study in all faculties. But whereas Harvard's concentrated on the humanities (32 of 44), the Yale students preferred the sciences by a small margin (18 of 31). Many of these scientists were graduates of Yale's Sheffield Scientific School, migrating to obtain a kind of education clearly impossible to receive at home. The relatively high proportion of students sent by New England colleges in the first five decades has an obvious curricular motive. A much higher percentage of these (37%, compared to 13% for Harvard and Yale) studied theology in Germany. Evidently, students from the relatively pious and God-fearing New England colleges were not deterred by any reputation for godlessness pertaining to German higher criticism.

By comparison, their interest in the other two professional faculties of law and medicine is noticeably smaller than Harvard's or the New York colleges'. Despite their differing theological positions, both Andover and Harvard Divinity schools sent a great many more students to Germany than either Union or Yale. The numbers from the Middle Atlantic state colleges are really too small to comment on. They have only 15 students in the sample, most (9) in the philosophical faculty. This region is, of course, underrepresented in the sample. But even if the numbers were doubled, they would not amount to all that much. The South's numbers are also small. In contrast to those from the Middle Atlantic states, the students from southern colleges seem to have preferred Germany's professional faculties, particularly law and medicine. Perhaps there was a motivation toward professional study abroad to avoid the just emerging professional schools of the North.

Whether or not this last speculation is justified, there is no doubt that southern students did postpone making their journey more than students from any other region. The proportion of students from Harvard who went to German universities within two years of college graduation or leaving professional school is more than twice as high (52 of 73, or 71%) as those from the South (4 of 15, or 27%). Yale students, too, although not quite as many of them managed to leave for Germany quite so quickly as those from Harvard, saw most (31 of 52, or 60%) going within two years after Commencement. But students from colleges in the New England, Middle Atlantic, and midwestern states often had to postpone their journeys considerably longer. Only half (23 of 46) from New England colleges could go immediately, and only four of the fifteen from the Middle Atlantic states. The rest had to wait for up to ten years to make their journeys abroad.

The only exception to this pattern of waiting was for students from New York colleges, 68 percent of whom (17 of 25) went to German universities within two years. Clearly, greater affluence, as well as exposure to German-trained professors at Harvard, Yale, and some New York colleges, had a great deal to do with the higher motivation of these students to migrate to Germany as quickly as they could. Students in these colleges may also have been more oriented to the new type of scholarship than those from more parochial institutions. It is also true that students from rural areas would have found it far more difficult to raise the relatively large amount of cash needed for the journey and for expenses in Germany. There is no report of anyone in this period having worked his way through a

German course of study (although some students did make extra money from tutoring their fellow Americans). All the money had to be raised in advance. It took many students as long as ten years to make it.

Although there was some information available on fathers' occupation and income range, this was not extensive enough to warrant any hard conclusions. What was found tended to indicate that most of these early students came from relatively affluent parents. Their fathers tended to be bankers or merchants or wealthy farmers. The sons of ministers or poor country doctors frequently had to raise the money for the cost of their German education through loans from relatives or by working for an extended period beforehand. Some, like G. S. Hall, owed their journeys to a wealthy benefactor, but this was rare.[20] The more usual means of finance for students whose parents could not pay was for the American college or university to advance or donate the money. Harvard was particularly generous in this regard.[21] Yale much less so, perhaps another result of the former's greater proportion of German-trained faculty in this period.

Oddly enough, despite the lowering of transatlantic fares in the 1840s and the continuing rise in the cost of living at home, both of which made the expense of German education relatively much lower at the end compared with the beginning of this period, the proportion of students going directly to Germany from college did not increase greatly. The percentage of students leaving within two years did go up from 58 percent (22 of 38) in the 1840s to 70 percent (39 of 56) in the 1850s. But in the following decade it dropped again to 63 percent (66 of 88). Perhaps this is only due to the Civil War, which may have made some students postpone their journeys, although it provided an incentive for others to go more quickly.

The decreasing (relative and absolute) cost of German study would have made it possible for an increasing number of less affluent students to make the journey, and this seems to have been the case. But the numbers are not extensive enough to say for sure. If there was an increasing number of poorer students, they may have had to wait longer than others, thus maintaining the time intervals of earlier decades.

Many of these less affluent students tended to come from

rural areas, increasingly from farther west. The figures, quoted above, on the college regions of students traveling to Germany exaggerated even more the predominance of the North and East. Many students from the South and the Midwest attended older colleges in the East. Over the six decades after 1810, the percentage of New England-born students declines somewhat from 61 percent to 51 percent (23 of 38 to 45 of 88), while the number of those from the Middle Atlantic states (including New York) increases from 26 percent to 39 percent. The number from the South peaks at 8 (of 76, or 10.5%) in the 1850s. Again, the numbers from the Midwest are too small to deal with.

The greatest migration of students from one region in America to attend college in another seems to have been from the Middle Atlantic states to New England. The numbers of these students increased in the 1850s and 1860s. This geographical mobility is obviously a good indicator of a greater likelihood of continuing their education in Germany. The affluence which permitted this initial mobility is also a consideration for the German pilgrimage.

Comparing the regions of origin to regions of final settlement, we find that there is a rather marked movement westward by students from New England and the Middle Atlantic states. The distortion of the sample may mask a corresponding movement of westerners east, but that seems unlikely. The westward movement parallels the migration of the general population in the period. Besides this movement, we might also note the migration from the South to the North (11 of 26 students) and the more or less permanent transplantation of more than 10 percent (25 of 245) students to Europe.

Many of the students who returned from Germany settled in more than one region. Students from both New England and the Middle Atlantic states tended to come back to their own region for a little while and then move on.

One of the reasons for their mobility may have been the slow pace of educational reform and the consequent small numbers of jobs available in settled areas. Despite the relatively sparse opportunities for college teaching in this period before the era of modern American universities, however, the majority of returning students from Germany elect an academic career. The proportion of these careers rises from 51 percent (21 of 41) in the period before 1840, to 62 percent (59 of 95) in the 1860s. The numbers of students enrolled in the law and medical faculties are roughly equal to those who subsequently became lawyers and doctors (27 and 31 respectively, compared to 25 and 26). The number of clergymen (29), however, is a good deal less than the 42 Americans who studied theology in Germany. Moreover, a large number of those who did become ordained, made at least some of their career in a university or theological school. The number of simple ministers is very small; obviously the German education did not encourage that kind of commitment. Yet, German higher criticism did not shake any large numbers from their faith.

Among the other professions, there are perhaps a few more businessmen (17) than might have been expected among a group whose education was as elevated and specialized as could be had in the nineteenth century. With the exception of Pierce Noble Welch (a notable Yale benefactor) and several Harvard overseers, most would have little to do with higher education again.

What we would like to gain from our sample, and really cannot, is the change within that category of "academic" within the span of our period. In terms of sheer numbers, the proportion of academics remains fairly constant to the total numbers of students and the total numbers of occupations throughout the whole time. But what does change lies behind the numbers in the people themselves. Among those in the first group that we have listed as having taken up an academic profession for at least some time after their return, we find the familiar names of George Bancroft, Joseph Green Cogswell, George Ticknor, and Henry W. Longfellow. Names like these are quite typical in the earlier period, despite the fact that by the standards of the latter half of the century their academic careers tended to be highly irregular, hardly academic careers at all in the accepted sense of the word. If these unusual people are subtracted from the list, only a small number remain who found positions in academic institutions as the major source of their livelihoods and who remained there for the greater part of their lives.

One of the very few who might be considered to have done

this was Robert Bridges Patton. A graduate of the Yale class of 1818, Patton studied philology at Göttingen just after Bancroft. It is not entirely certain, but he appears to have been the second American recipient (after Bancroft) of an earned German Ph.D.[22] Upon his return home about 1822, he took successive positions as a teacher of Greek in several schools and colleges. By 1826 he was Professor of Greek at Princeton, a position which he left in 1834 to assume a post at the newly established University of the City of New York. The latter decision marks him as among a very small number of real educational reformers in higher education, as the new university was dedicated to a new idea of teaching and research much closer than anything else in America to the German conception of the university.

Patton died within two years of actually joining the new university in 1838, and before he had made much of a name for himself either as an educational reformer or a scholar. Within the context of his time both he and his career were anomalies. But from the perspective of the later development of the academic profession and the American universities, his career was far more paradigmatic than Bancroft's. The number of career patterns like his grows substantially in the 1850s and 1860s, while the proportion of independent mavericks like Bancroft steadily declines.

The twofold increase in the number of academic careers in the decade of the 1840s is the numerical sign of this change. Although the fifties and sixties still had their learned and independent outsiders—men like Horace Furness, who never held a university post and yet was reputed to be the best Shakespearean authority of his day—academic scholars such as Francis Child and William Dwight Whitney began to be far more typical.

The changing composition of the returning students who followed "other" professions is yet another indication of the normalization of careers and the emergence of postgraduate education as a form of professional training. In the first half of the nineteenth century, students in this category tended to be wealthy and independent. If they worked at all, they did not usually derive their livelihoods from their work and did not always follow one career. But students from the last two decades tend to have more regular employment patterns, and to derive most of their living from their work and follow only one occupation for most of their lives. Newspaper or magazine writing[23] or editing were perhaps more typical occupations for those in this group who had studied the humanities in the 1850s or 1860s. Scientists often became government or private geologists or industrial chemists. Thus, even within the category there is a perceptible movement toward greater normalization of career preparation and specialization, as was the case in university professions.

Within the academic profession itself there are still other signs of this trend. One concrete piece of evidence was the growing number of Ph.Ds. In the first decades students were relatively indifferent toward actually standing for the degree even if they had fulfilled all of the requirements. A great number simply did not bother to get the Ph.D. even though they had been in residence for three or four years. Although nearly one-quarter of the American students in our sample received the degree, most of these studied in Germany in the last two decades of our period. And many of those who did not, still managed to do research and publish in their fields after their return.

Besides the growth of institutions in business, government, and the academic world, the nineteenth century also witnessed great changes in preparation and careers in law, medicine, and theology, the three traditional vocations for which a higher education was required. The period also witnessed the emergence of new academic professions in the humanities and sciences. And these new vocations also shared the same tendencies toward an increasingly rigid professional preparation, specialization, hierarchical social and professional organization, and standardized career patterns that marked many other nineteenth-century middle-class occupations. In America these changes in the humanities and sciences are intimately connected to the migration of American students to the German universities and the sense of scholarship and the vocation of scholarship that many appear to have acquired there.

Yet this does not seem to have been an automatic or an easy acquisition; nor does it appear to have begun with the very first Americans who studied there. We have examined a sample of the students who studied in Germany from 1810 to 1870.

We have seen who many of them were, where they came from, where they studied, and where they returned. We have looked at what they studied in Germany and what they did on their return. But we have not seen yet how much or what they actually learned or what they brought back of their hard-won German education.

We have seen that many more students up to 1870 studied the humanities rather than the sciences in Germany. Most of the former group learned something that went by the name of "philology." What they learned of it is difficult to know. Very few of them became academic philologists in the German sense of that calling. But many of them, just as much as the scientists, derived from their studies a sense of philology and of academic study in the humanities as a legitimate and authentic vocation, and one which required not only their own allegiance in many cases, but which also demanded the support of specialized institutions of higher education and research that were wholly unbuilt and almost unimagined when they returned to America. It is this generation of students who returned from German study before 1870 which fashioned both the institutions of higher learning and the ideas and criteria for higher learning in the humanities.

CHAPTER 4

I am exceedingly anxious to have this spirit of pursuing all literary studies philosophically—of making scholarship as little of drudgery and mechanism as possible, transplanted to the U. States, in whose free and liberal soil I think it would, at once, find congenial nourishment.

—George Ticknor to Thomas Jefferson

The Anxieties of Influence:
The First Generation of American Students in German Universities

How did the first group of American students in the German universities assimilate the scholarship they found there, and how much did they assimilate? If they could not or would not imitate the German scholars or their work, precisely why was that? Was it only because they could not understand what the Germans were saying or perceive how it was new? Could they not appreciate its importance? Was it because every single one of them had theological blinkers on?

Some of these questions can be answered easily and quickly. Even the more superficial and less well-prepared of the Americans gained some knowledge of what the Germans were doing and how they did it. The clearest example of this is how they perceived the importance and understood the breakthroughs in classical philology made by Friedrich August Wolf. Almost as soon as they were off the packet boat the Americans were made well aware of his reputation and achievements. And despite all the scandalous stories of his domestic tyranny, laziness, and vituperation, they were impressed.[1] "The Coryphaeus of Philologians, the Ishmael of criticism," both Ticknor and Everett proclaim him.[2] And both take him very seriously indeed, working through the *Prolegomena ad Homerum* slowly and carefully. When George Bancroft arrived a few years later he, too, had to apply himself. "In Philology, Wolf & yet Wolf & yet Wolf,"[3] he complained—but he kept on reading. The other Americans did likewise. Three years after he had worked eighteen hours a day to decipher the *Prolegomena,* Everett wrote to Bancroft to send him another copy: "I have sent home one copy, but want another."[4]

Did the Americans understand what they spent so much time reading? This is somewhat harder to judge; but the evidence seems to indicate that they did. Everett wrote an exceedingly detailed and comprehensive series of lectures on the book.[5] These demonstrate that he at least understood Wolf thoroughly. The other Americans, when they learned the new methods of scansion, remembered that through these techniques Wolf was able to determine the authenticity of large sections of the *Iliad*. When they learned how to use etymology to evaluate texts critically, they knew that Wolf was able to restore ancient texts with its help.[6] Thus, the indications are that if the American students might not always have mastered specific philological techniques, they understood their importance and use.

But did the Americans really respect what the German scholars had achieved? Did they appreciate the value of these philological discoveries? Here again the evidence seems clearly to indicate that they did. Although they were far from loath to complain of the tedium of philological work, they were quick to assert the necessity of these endeavors. Everett emphasized his "respect for this part of the business."[7] And after having denigrated Wolf's character for more than two years, Bancroft willingly admitted:

He is a genius of the first order; one of the few great men whom it has been my lot to meet with in Germany [he had already met Goethe, Wilhelm von Humboldt, and Schleiermacher, among many others]. Hated by his countrymen, he consoles himself with being the most learned man on the Continent. He has a fondness for the ancient languages, & is alive to the beauties of their literature.[8]

Thus Bancroft, one of the most severe critics of German scholarship and the German academic system, conceded that the philologian's work did not prevent him from enjoying the material he analyzed. His was *not* the Wordsworthian lament, "We murder to dissect."

Finally, did the Americans assimilate this German scholarship? Did they bring back this painfully acquired classical philology and practice the Wolfian techniques in the American colleges that so many of them taught in? Here the evidence is clear and unequivocal: they did not.

We must wonder if they were really sincere in their admiration for Wolf's achievements. And if so, it is curious that there were no scholars like him among the first group of American students in the German universities. Was every one of the dozens of able and intelligent Americans in this group unsuited for this work? Then why did so many of them become college teachers on their return?

In the rosy-hued world of the historiography of American education, where bright-eyed, brilliant ephebes sit eternally at the feet of avuncular professors, opposition to change tends to be portrayed in purely external forms: reactionary presidents, tight-fisted legislatures. It is the received opinion that those Americans who were actually exposed to the new German scholarship in the humanities (theology is a different story)[9] became firm and committed converts and that they were frustrated only by the opposition of those who did not go. Thus Samuel Morison exclaims of the first Americans at Göttingen that "a new world of scholarship opened up before the delighted gaze of these four men."[10] And David Tyack claims, "As academic missionaries, Ticknor, Everett, Bancroft, and Cogswell all returned to Harvard hoping to show Americans the meaning of scholarship and culture."[11]

Now this is partly true. These four men did return with a certain amount of messianic zeal. But they were not converts to the German form of scholarship in the humanities. Not one of them came back a real classical philologist or anything else that the Germans of the day would have recognized as a scholar. Russell Nye asserts that "Everett's years of foreign study paid back Harvard tenfold."[12] But it is difficult to see how. Everett only taught for a few years at Harvard, and achieved no lasting influence there. He never wrote anything that was considered a work of scholarship—even in America. And he did virtually nothing for the cause of educational reform in his years as president of Harvard. Thomas Wentworth Higginson's statement that the influence of Everett and his companions "both on Harvard University and on American education was enormous,"[13] is pure speechmaking.

Yet some modern historians, admitting the lack of lasting effect of these "literary pioneers" (as Orie Long dubbed them), still claim that they themselves enjoyed and profited from their period of German study. Cynthia Brown asserts, "Everett and Bancroft had a splendid time of it."[14] Sometimes they did. Quite often they did not.

Did they learn anything? Some historians have noted that the first American students at Göttingen did not feast unreservedly at the banquet of learning spread before them there. The reason for this, it is claimed, was that the Americans were offended by the personal habits and immorality of the professors with whom they came into contact. David Tyack writes:

The Yankees respected the intellectual accomplishments of the German scholars, but a note of nostalgia for home, of a desire for the society which Mrs. Perkins [a Boston correspondent] represented, of distaste for the poor manners and corrupt opinions of German scholars, of condescension even, runs through the letters and journals of Ticknor and his friends during their stay in Germany.[15]

All of the above is certainly true enough. But it does not explain the real reaction of Americans to German study. If a dislike of German morality and society were all these men objected to, one could expect that their antipathy would not extend to German scholarship itself.

Virtually every one of the first Americans came to Germany with the best of intentions. Something happened to every one of them in the German universities which changed their longing to make themselves into real scholars. They did not change for reasons associated with opposition or lack of facilities in America. Rather, their opposition was personal and internal.

This reaction of American students to German universities and scholarship must in large part have grown out of their German experience. But there is in many of them an initial ambivalence and set of expectations which colored that experience and which help to explain the later reaction.

The American interest in German scholars and scholarship was comparatively sudden and intense, and from the beginning provoked a cerain anxiety. On August 12, 1812, Moses Stuart, the already formidable Andover theologian,[16] wrote to the young Harvard graduate Edward Everett extolling Herder and German theology. He invited the young man to come up to Andover and peruse his collection of German books: "You shall take as many as you please. I want to make you undertake to translate Herder."[17]

Thus Stuart inaugurated a correspondence and a carefully tended friendship which quickly led to Everett's mastery of German and his immersion in the work of the impious but pioneering German theologian, Eichhorn. Stuart was not in the least circumspect about his plans for Everett. When the latter was on the point of accepting the Brattle Street congregation, Stuart wrote with an indelicacy that was only usual:

I understand that you are soon to preach & probably to be settled. I must take the liberty to express my doubt, whether you ought to stop in your present course, so much short as parochial duties will compel you to do. You will be obliged to put off many pleasant studies, which at your time of life, will be a sore trial.[18]

Yet, even after an unmistakable hint from Everett that his ardor in fulfilling Stuart's ambitions may have been somewhat less than Stuart's own, the older man persisted in his urgings. A few months after Everett had accepted his Brattle Street pulpit, Stuart renewed his campaign to turn him to a scholarly vocation, remarking with pointed emphasis: "Is it not wonderful that this country has never yet produced a work in sacred literature, which can lay claim to some importance."[19] Nine months later Stuart was still on the same theme, still unheedful of Everett's commitment to the pastoral vocation:

But I know your ardour in this noble cause, & I trust, know how to value it. Who may despair that we may yet have some select, Oriental chair, which may do something that shall deserve respect at home & abroad.[20]

The chauvinist anxiety and appeal is too naked even for Stuart; he immediately qualifies it: "This is not indeed to be regarded as the motive of action."[21] But the disclaimer only aggravates the suspicions aroused by the insistence and vehemence of that which it denies. However impure even Stuart regarded doing "something that shall deserve respect" as a motive for action, its power was undeniable. Doing "something that shall deserve respect at home and abroad" was indeed a principal "motive of action" of the first Americans who sought to assimilate the new German scholarship, not least of them Edward Everett.

It was not a "select, Oriental chair" which moved Everett from the pulpit (where he had been wildly successful) to the Göttingen library, but a new, mysterious (an anonymous donor) endowment for a classical scholar. Everett permitted himself to

be considered, and not surprisingly was chosen. He departed for
the uncharted German wilderness with the usual pioneer optimism and innocence, and the rhetoric of his first letters to his
friends is unrestrained in its praise of German scholarship:
"Seriously, if you would read Greek or Latin with unmingled
edification," he wrote to Theodore Lyman,

> you would do well to spend your leisure time for the next six months on
> the German language; which from the humblest grammar up to the highest
> commentary, is for its store of critical aids, as far before England, as
> England before America,—and I can use no stronger illustration. The idea
> that everything German is tediously prolix and dull, is one of the most
> absurd prejudices I know. There are more manuals, abridgments, popular
> views, and every sort of device to make learning attractive and easy, than
> in all other languages, yea, there are better accounts of English literature,
> than are to be found in any English work.[22]

The Germans already appear to have had an unenviable reputation in the New World. Everett attempts to refute it. He does it
by attempting to show the relevance of German scholarship and
even its popular appeal. He seemingly opens himself unreservedly to the Germans and their form of scholarship, proclaiming
them intellectual and moral allies against the insufferable English. This use of the Germans as potential cultural allies against
the English is a particularly potent appeal in this early period.

> Dr. Burney . . . after having spent twenty years on arranging the choruses
> of aschylus [*sic*] , is pronounced by Boeckh, in a famous new Pindar, to
> be singularly unlucky in proposing to introduce a new series of metre,
> into the last Author, just after it had been happily exploded by Her-
> mann. Now though this is certainly insolence, and German insolence is
> as offensive as any other, yet it remains, I think an indisputable fact,
> that the number and extent of their philological researches, far exceed
> everything of which the English can make a boast. I confess I sit down
> very humbly and study their Latin grammars.[23]

Everett is ready to forgive German insolence, not simply because it is German or anti-British but because he thinks it
justified, justified by the power and authority of the German
academic system. Everett proclaims himself content "to sit
down very humbly and study their Latin grammars." In other
words, a man of considerable worldly achievement and success
was ready to sit like a schoolboy to learn the new German

scholarship. He admits freely the power of the German system and appears to open himself completely to it.

Yet, even then Everett was by no means so accepting and committed as he often made himself appear. For, as he wrote to his brother shortly after arriving at Göttingen:

My appointment to Cambridge, which has changed my situation and prospects, so entirely, was hardly an object of my expectation a month before it took place. And I do not feel myself, to have got into just my place, though I confess that I do not know any other likely to be accessible.[24]

Nonetheless, Everett set out in his studies with a fervor that was little short of heroic. And he made considerable progress, impressing all who knew him as a singularly intelligent and immensely hardworking student. He began by studying both classical and biblical philology, enrolling in the theologian Eichhorn's classes to master the philological techniques which the eminent critic had pioneered. Yet, by the end of his first year of study, he harbors a curious pessimism about his studies that contrasts markedly with his actual progress, as well as with his teachers' opinions of his work:

I am giving myself very exclusively to Latin and Greek and make some progress in each. I get along beyond my expectations in the Greek metres and am sometimes able to arrange a passage of Aeschylus, *in curia libariorum* [?] *valde turbatum.* And what is better, I have more respect for this part of the business, than I thought I should, since I am convinced that it has been a great means of keeping pure, and may be of restoring, the older Greek poets. I wish you could see my Dissen's [Everett's Göttingen Greek professor] Homer, it looks like a bundle of old rags, or at least a favorite novel from a circulating library. He says he has read it in order through ten times: each time investigating some particular point, and he quotes it from Memory as an aged Minister does the bible.—I find I have begun too late even to begin to go into the thing as they do here, but I get what they call an aesthetical view of the subject, which is more adapted to the American market, though I should be glad to have put myself on a footing with the critics here. It moves my imagination when I think how much money and time are wasted with us on, what they call an education.[25]

This rather surprising passage begins with an apparently optimistic statement of Everett's progress—which had been considerable. He frankly acknowledges the worth and authenticity of a more esoteric and painstaking form of German scholarship and describes his teacher's devotion to scholarship with the approving simile of the old minister quoting from memory from the Bible. Up to this point there is no hint that Everett is not fully satisfied with what he is doing and fully committed to realizing this level of scholarship himself. Yet, he shifts abruptly and without explanation from this initial optimism and warm admission of the value of German scholarship to an almost bitter pessimism and disavowal of it for him. He gives no indication of anything that might have prompted this shift. The reasons he uses to justify it are too abrupt and gratuitous to be credible or realistic. He does not say that he no longer wants to be a scholar. On the contrary, he asserts that he still "should be glad to place myself on a footing with the critics here." And he does not offer any evidence of incapacity to do just that. He was thought perhaps the most brilliant man in New England. And his German teachers certainly respected his intelligence as well as his capacity for hard work.[26] The other reason that he offered, the need to adapt his subject to the supposed demands of the American market, would have been a very real threat to anyone *except* Everett. His position was not only assured, it also gave more scope for going beyond an "aesthetical view" of classical studies than any other college post in America. Everett was well aware even before he got to Germany how lacking America was in libraries and learned journals. But he never once cites that lack as a reason for his own abrupt reversal.

Everett's disaffection is a puzzling psychological phenomenon, and one that is not explained by commonsense "reasons" which cite the conditions of study in Germany and America. Moreover, as abrupt and puzzling as his disavowal of classical scholarship was, it must also have been genuine and profound. From that time forth he confined himself almost exclusively to learning languages:[27] Arabic, Modern Greek, French, and Italian. He never again immersed himself in philology.

Nor did Everett ever offer a real explanation for his sudden reversal. As we have seen, there were not unhidden reservations in his attitude toward Germany and scholarship from the very beginning. At any rate, he was not always as enthusiastic as has sometimes been alleged. Was this merely Everett's personal preference, his own assessment of his capabilities and interests? Partly it must be. Yet Everett's expectations and his conception of the role of scholars and scholarship was at least partly culturally derived. American culture was deeply divided about the value of the new German learning. And it transmitted that sense of division in extremely subtle and intricate psychological games. In Everett's case, these games are often hidden from the historical record. But for George Bancroft, his younger and less sophisticated successor in Germany, they are terrifyingly present.

Bancroft, like Everett, was sent to Germany through the generosity—and insistence—of John Kirkland. Precocious and able, Bancroft lacked Everett's assurance and sense of superiority. His first letter to Everett reveals the confusion and anxiety produced by Kirkland's instructions:

My course of studies must also be regulated by my friends at home, & by a reconsideration of what will most contribute to rendering me useful on my return. The wishes of Dr. Kirkland, so far as they are expressed, would be superior to all other considerations. These, however, he has never fully communicated. In his letter he has given me for Professor Eichhorn, he observes of me that 'His friends wish him to attend especially to Philology, the ancient languages, & Oriental literature, that he may thus be qualified to pursue theological studies to the greatest benefit, to give instruction as any opening may occur and invite, & become an accomplished philologian & Biblical critic, able to expound & defend the oracles of God.' Dr. Kirkland has also told me, that I should not give my time so exclusively to critical studies as to unfit myself for a clergyman, since it is at least doubtful whether the University will ever have occasion to demand of me any services. The primary object of my studies must therefore be, to gain the ancient languages, & I hope a few hours which my leisure & repose will give me such of the modern languages as are worth the acquiring.[28]

If the complaint Bancroft mentions was real, it must have posed a real dilemma for him. For Kirkland had *not* said not to go to Germany; nor had the president enjoyed him not to learn the higher criticism. Kirkland was responsible for sending Bancroft there in the first place, and for committing a large sum of the corporation's money to doing so. He is not, according to this passage, even worried about Bancroft's coming home contaminated with infidelity; the young man's orthodoxy is simply assumed. He did not say, do not become a good scholar. On the contrary, he urges Bancroft to become as good a scholar as he can be. Yet Kirkland apparently also said "it is at least doubtful if the University will ever have occasion to demand . . . any services." This appears to have been a very real source of Bancroft's anxiety.

Why would Kirkland send this youth three thousand miles at great expense to study for three or four years, and all for nothing, not even the possibility of a job? The New England respect for learning did not yet extend to such acts. Why must he become "an accomplished philologian" if the arduous and expensive training this would require would almost certainly be wasted in a clergyman's vocation that could have been had without any of this bother? It does not make sense. Either Bancroft had exaggerated or twisted Kirkland's words, or Kirkland was operating with very mixed motives. The latter appears more likely. Because the absence of reward—the prestigious position and career that Bancroft so craved—did not appear to be at all related to anything that the young man did, he found himself in a psychologically real, and terrifying, double bind (in a clinical sense). It does not make a great deal of difference if the bind was intentional or not; it was indisputably real for Bancroft. The young man's intense anxiety is hardly surprising.

Several weeks after his first letter to Everett and the latter's only partially reassuring response, Bancroft wrote again, his anxieties undiminished. He posed a dilemma with which he was to torture himself and his friends for the next two years:

To understand the Hebrew Bible thoroughly & critically, two or three at the least other languages must be learned; and these would give me so much occupation, that philology must become quite a secondary affair. Or on the other hand, I may give myself up to the classical literature & at the same time resign the hope of doing much at interpreting the Scripture. A question thus arises in my mind whether after gaining a fair degree of acquaintance with the Classics, & that chiefly in view of undertaking them, I should strike off into the wide region of Oriental literature?[29]

The whole problem of studying classical philology appears to be a new problem. Kirkland had intended that he devote some of his time to that discipline. But this is the first hint that Bancroft might prefer to give himself wholly to it. Had he decided that theology was simply too difficult—or too loaded—to risk his precious time at Göttingen at it? But how could he avoid striking "off into the wide region of Oriental literature" if that was what he had been sent to do? This, in effect, was what Everett wrote back to his young friend.

There is another dimension to Bancroft's request which relates it more directly to the bind he was in with Kirkland. The same week that Bancroft wrote to Everett, he also penned a letter to his old mentor, Andrews Norton:

Life is short, the time we pass on earth is but a speck.... Shall I devote myself to gaining a fairly intimate acquaintance with L. [atin] and G. [reek] , an acquaintance not unworthy of a scholar, or shall I only touch at this port and then go into the wide sea of orientalism? Who at Cambridge knows the languages of the East? Have you one thorough critic even in Hebrew? But in the same degree that the attention is diverted to them, must be the value of the acquaintance. What good would it do me or those about me if I knew as much of them as Eichhorn if I found nobody who cared for them? And must not my sole reward be a sweet but secret satisfaction? And yet I feel a strong sentiment, that urges me to study the languages of the East.[30]

The strong sentiment that urged the study of the languages of the East was called John Kirkland, who also threatened that the sole reward for this knowledge and the years of hard study needed to acquire it would be a "sweet but secret satisfaction."

Bancroft implies in this letter that only theological learning and knowledge of the ancient languages would be penalized by lack of appreciation and use in America. But that is not a distinction which Kirkland had made in his letter, in which all learning, classical or biblical, had little chance of being of service to the university. Philology was seen only as a possible hindrance to the performance of pastoral duties. Bancroft, however, converts this into a fear of the danger of theological study alone. "The wide region of Oriental literature" and the "wide sea of orientalism" become trigger words of his anxiety. And he changes what had been a double bind directed at higher learning and philological scholarship as a whole, into a specific fear about theology.

A few weeks later Bancroft appeared to reverse himself. Despite the obvious preference for classical studies to biblical philology, in his first letter to Norton he wrote:

How have my views changed since I left Boston; then I thought only of becoming well versed in Philology, and hearing a few courses on General

literature, which would improve me as a scholar and as a gentleman;
and now I would fain become a thorough theologian.[31]

This is *not* what Bancroft had told his friends before leaving
home, and certainly not what he had told Kirkland. Nor,
indeed, was it what he wrote to Everett before he had even
arrived at Göttingen. The very terms of the corporation's sending him to Germany had been to give him a *thorough* grounding
in biblical criticism, to make him into "a thorough theologian."[32] It most certainly was not merely to improve him" as
a scholar and a gentleman" or to allow him to audit a few
courses "on General literature"; nor was there any way in the
world that Bancroft could have been honestly ignorant of or
mistaken about Kirkland's or the corporation's intentions.

What had been set down on paper, even recorded in the
official records of Harvard College, was not something that it
was easy to forget or contradict, at least not to people as
familiar with the truth as Bancroft's correspondents. Yet, Bancroft evidently felt anxious enough to disregard these considerations. His psychological game has a certain desperate quality.

None of Bancroft's friends offered him much relief. Despite
the clear implication of his letter to Everett that he would be
glad of any excuse to abandon his Oriental studies, the older
man was not going to let him off the hook:

Every man on these points, must finally judge for himself. I agree with
the Gentlemen at Göttingen that three years is little eno' to give to either,
as the Primal study, not to say, by this—as they do not say—that you are
positively to pay no attention to any collateral study whatsoever. On the
contrary, there is such an affinity between the studies of profane &
sacred criticism that they intertwine each other. But still it will be necessary to choose one as a first pursuit; and for reasons wh' I will state, I
think the Oriental languages as applied or applicable to Sacred literature
most worthy of yr attention.[33]

This was a mature, though waffling response, and unremarkable
except that it happened to come from someone who had
already personally rejected every one of the reasons he was
about to offer Bancroft. Not only that, but his insistence on
the compatibility of the two studies dodged the whole issue.
Bancroft had not implied that he wished absolutely to choose
between one or the other. Nor had he implied that by choosing

the one he would necessarily have to abandon the other. In fact, he had written to Norton that he would at the very least "touch at this Port" of classical studies even if he gave himself to theology.

Not only did Everett ignore Bancroft's wishes as well as his words, but he also gave him a point of view that he himself had rejected for more than personal reasons. He urged the study of theology for the younger man when not long before he had condemned the whole discipline in bitter words:

> But I tremble to think I had come to giving credit to that poorest of all systematizing, systematic Theology, of which the very terms are now loathsome to me. . . . I shall content myself with hammering upon the Greek, and leave the world to fight out the cause of religion as piously as they have fought it out hitherto.[34]

Everett, in other words, was recommending a course of study which he had found to be not only uncongenial but worthless.

Nevertheless, Bancroft did not know this, and for the moment submitted to Everett's arguments:

> As your advice in respect to my studies coincides with my own inclinations, and I trust also to the expectations of my friends, I can no longer have any doubts respecting the course I must adopt.[35]

The assertion that Everett's advice only confirms Bancroft's own inclinations is an interesting psychological subterfuge,[36] though one cannot judge whether it was more effective against Everett or against Bancroft himself. Not only is the statement minutely subverted by the compulsive language of the last phrases, but it is absolutely contradicted by what he had written to Norton only a week before. That Bancroft now appears to have little difficulty determining "the expectations of my friends," belies the complaint of his first letter to Everett that these expectations had never been communicated fully. This point is confirmed a few months later when Bancroft writes to Kirkland, "Your wish I believe, was, that I should study with the thought in mind, that I am to be for my life, a student of theology."[37]

The certainty that Bancroft had assured Everett necessarily flowed from this knowledge of what was expected appears to have evaporated. Bancroft troubles Kirkland with the very same issue that he had told Everett was definitively settled.[38] Since Kirkland had already told him (more than once) that he wished Bancroft to become a "student of theology," and since that was really (as he had assured both Kirkland and Everett) what Bancroft himself wanted, there should have been no problem. Why, then, is there a problem?

If Bancroft did not like his work, it is difficult to see why he did not say so. Kirkland asked him to do that. The suspicion that Bancroft is begging for any kind of sanction to make the same switch to classical studies and languages that Everett had made is strengthened a few lines farther down in his letter to Kirkland:

I have said, I believe, enough to be intelligible. I will conform myself to your advice, & I pray that you will favour me with it, by the first opportunity. I add one word about German Theology. I have nothing to do with it except so far as it is merely *critical.* Of the infidel systems I hear not a word, and I trust I have been too long under your eye, and too long a member of the Theological Institution under your inspection to be in danger of being led away from the religion of my Fathers.[39]

Since Kirkland's advice had already been given—repeatedly—on this point, what Bancroft was asking for was different advice. Moreover, as if to underscore the implicit danger of forcing someone into theological study, the specter of infidelity is raised by Bancroft himself. There was at least an implicit threat in this "word about German Theology" that is appended so immediately following an inarticulated request. That, in any case, was the way in which Kirkland understood this letter from his "dear boy." Yet, even though Bancroft had said more than enough "to be intelligible," the president was not ready to yield, or at least to take the first step:

It was expected that you should pursue a line of study connected with theology, but not exclusively. If you wish to relinquish this course; & to have more scope, I would have you say so. But it would be very satisfactory & very useful, to have you thoroughly versed in the oriental department, provided that it would not expose you to any other evil. Our friend, Professor Stuart, is very desirous that you should sit awhile at the feet of Gesenius, the Professor [of theology] at Halle.[40]

Kirkland explicity said that Bancroft could give up theology if he wished, although the president made it plain that both he and Stuart would prefer Bancroft to continue that course. Yet, just a few days after receiving this letter Bancroft was writing to Everett again:

The good people at home, I am afraid, will not like to have me give myself to German Theology too closely. They have written to me they would be well content, if I abandoned that science, & devoted myself to any other branch.[41]

Bancroft may have had another correspondent whose name and letter he did not record in his rather extensive list. But it is most likely that he was referring to Kirkland's statement that if he wished to change his course, it would be best to say so. However, if Kirkland was indeed "the good people back home" to whom Bancroft referred, then the young man was playing a very deceitful—or desperate—game.[42] Kirkland had most certainly *not* urged him not to study theology, just the opposite. Again, this was an exceedingly reckless thing to say to someone who had precisely the correspondents to put the lie to such an assertion.

By this time Bancroft had asked nearly every one of his numerous American correspondents for advice on whether to study theology or classics. Yet, he had begun his letter to Everett with the conspiratorial introduction: "There are a great many things about which I wish to take counsel with you, & you are the only one well able to give it me."[43] Since this came after a year of repeating precisely the same question, the older man must have felt somewhat annoyed, though he replied with his usual graciousness:

Tho' a good deal of apprehension—that not altogether unfounded—is felt, at home, of the tenets of German theology, you need not be frightened on that score. You will certainly be able to distinguish between what is to be held to & what rejected. . . .[44]

This was putting the matter with uncharacteristic bluntness. One did not have to operate with the slipperiness of a John Kirkland to survive in Federalist Boston. If a certain measure of common sense, and Bancroft possessed that, was sufficient to discern the limits of orthodoxy, then the issue was a simple one, in fact so simple as to make Bancroft's protestations most suspicious. The theological issue was being used as a cover.

Everett had called Bancroft at his game by responding with an unanswerable solution: distinguish between what you learn and what you teach, and keep your encounters with heterodoxy private. In addition, he assured Bancroft:

you need be under no fear, that you will not be able to bring y'r theology & languages to a good outlet in America. You need have no fear about not finding an honourable & respectable place there, whenever you come home & I could rather wish you, while abroad, to cultivate those studies for which our country affords least facility & most requires new aids.[45]

Coming from the Eliot Professor of Greek at Harvard, whose power over Kirkland and the corporation Bancroft had remarked often enough before, this was as close to an absolute guarantee of the first opening in theology as was possible.

Bancroft, however, seems at this time to have worked himself into an emotional state which may not have been susceptible to this kind of reassurance. He pleaded with Norton:

I wrote to you immediately after becoming a little at home in Göttingen, begging advice on my line of studies. The answer to this I awaited with longing anxiety. I expected to have your response at least 6 months ago, but time obliges me to decide for myself. Or rather, (*which is most decidedly fatal*) I remain as yet not fully decided [italics Bancroft's] .[46]

Why does Bancroft state that time has forced him to decide and then say that he has not yet fully decided? The new semester was months away, why all the sudden pressure for a decision? The statement that his present state of not having fully decided is "decidedly fatal" is almost hysterical. Norton had indicated repeatedly that he expected Bancroft to do what he had been sent to Göttingen to do, study theology; there was no reason for him to have changed his expectation. Nothing about the situation had altered. The only reason for Norton to change his mind was Bancroft's insistent repetition of the same question. The conclusion suggests itself that what Bancroft was asking for was not advice but the ratification of his own feelings, ratification which had to precede the open declaration of those feelings.

It seems clear that Bancroft underwent some kind of psychological struggle in his confrontation with German scholarship, and that he used the theological issue as a screen in a complicated psychological game.[47] His behavior is partly the expression of his own personal character and anxieties.[48] It takes two to play these kinds of games, however, and Bancroft never lacked for opponents. Kirkland and Everett appear to have participated fully in the complex psychological transactions. Bancroft's was a culturally derived and shared game.

Bancroft had come to Göttingen with rather grandiose notions of his own and the national destiny intermingled.[49] Into his vision of Columbia Triumphant he interpolated a conception of philological scholarship as the means for the cultural fulfillment of the new Republic, a transatlantic Greece:

Who does not also see that the literature of a kingdom is by no means calculated to preserve in its purity & force the republican spirit? We must then have a literature of our own. From the surplus of our treasury we must endow Universities, establish Libraries, patronize genius, and raise up in . . . [illegible] of men who may guide education, give the tone to society, disseminate taste & love of literature, & give our country the same mental as physical education. On what shall American literature be founded? Solely on the Classics—on that which we have in common with every nation in the world; nay, rather that which is in peculiar manner our own. The remains of the republics of antiquity are a rich legacy for the republics of modern times. To them do they more particularly belong. The country that is free should above all others hold in esteem the works of freedom. It is at the funeral pyre of Greece that the genius of American literature should light her torch.[50]

This brand of republican rhetoric which linked the destinies of the ancients to that of the new American nation was by no means original. Nor is the conjunction of this rhetorical flourish with classical scholarship and a new system of university education unique; that, after all, was what Jefferson had in mind for the University of Virginia. What was new was the linking of the classical inspiration to the new form of scholarship developed in Germany, and specifically to the new classical philology of Wolf and his successors. Classical scholarship was to be the pyre at which "the genius of American literature should light her torch." What is also noteworthy is that Bancroft should have begun with this vision, after he had begun to read the Germans but before he commenced his studies.

Bancroft gave forceful expression to his initial vision of the role of philology. It was not his vision alone, however, Kirkland and the Harvard corporation had sent him to Germany for precisely such a purpose. His words are wilder and more personal, but he echoes the aspirations of many others of the first generation of Americans to study in Germany when he says:

No sir; I have not left all that is dear to me; I have come to the land of learning, of literature, of science; and are not those dear to me? I have come to the pure fountains of wisdom, that I may drink of her unpolluted waters & be refreshed. 'Nonsense folly,' you are ready to exclaim. 'Do you think Eichhorn will give you waters of life clean & funning: Or will Hebrew & Greek help you to happiness & comfort? Or such lives improve your mind, & add to your usefulness?' Indeed I cannot answer from so great a distance. My voice must die away before it reached you. So I will only console myself with the words that the good angel of Columbus (if he had one) whispered in his ear "Steer west, Columbus, boldly to the west & you will certainly find land.' Where is the prodigal, that would give his tomorrow for Homer's eternity?[51]

Youthful exuberance and openness aside. Bancroft's language captures precisely the spirit of mercantile Boston embracing a new vision of republican prosperity and culture. The "prodigal, that would give his tomorrow for Homer's eternity" was an American whose passage east to study philology had been paid.

As we have seen, however, the commitment was not wholehearted. Bancroft's excited rhetoric and intemperate opinions were certainly an expression of his own peculiar character. They also expressed the divided opinion of his patrons. Bancroft certainly recognized that a mature and objective attitude was possible toward the Germans and their petty foibles.[53] Intellectually it was not beyond him. But he gave in constantly to the temptations to retail gossip and satisfy the almost prurient interest of Kirkland and his other correspondents.[54] He saw the better way, and he could not restrain himself from taking the worse:

I am afraid that you will think me a very scandalous fellow for telling so many tales out of school, and laughing at many people, and saying so little of ye works and virtues of Germans, who have been so kind to me, or have meant to be so. You must not believe all that I say. I am apt to make sweeping assertions, and to predicate absolutely what is only true when qualified. Thus though I may not love the land of the learned, I certainly wonder at them, and tho' I cannot value them very highly for moral feeling, they still have very vigorous understandings, and tho' the style of most German books is tedious, and void of beauty, still the matter contained in them is wonderfully deep. A spirit of learning pervades everything. Their works teem with citations, and have at least the merit for the most part of being written by men who are masters of their subject.[54]

This would seem to be balanced and mature judgment, a synthesis of his initial enthusiasm for German learning combined with an appreciation of its limits. In fact, it corresponds closely to Bancroft's initial conception[55] of classical studies as the proper domain of the new Republic rather than the corrupt old monarchies. Yet Bancroft found it impossible to sustain this balanced view within the context of his relationship to Kirkland. The problem is, can one constantly denigrate what one acknowledges to be the only means to intellectual and cultural authenticity without denying the authenticity itself? This was the constant unspoken dilemma of Bancroft's denunciation of the German professors and the university system of which they were a part. As he wrote to President Kirkland:

so I visited this & that German Professor; but what are German Professors to me? They have no time to spend for foreigners: He who can instruct me best in Greek metres, is a man, who has not found time from his studies to ask if there be a God, or a world in which we are to act. He, who can teach me to understand Horace, does not know that there are such things as morality and good manners.[56]

The moral criteria which Bancroft applies to his professors and their work not only deny moral but also intellectual validity to German scholarship. The professors were acknowledged as the only source of advanced knowledge of Greek metres and Horace. Thus, when Bancroft asks what the people who can help him understand Greek metres or Horace are to him, he is also asking what Horace or Greek metres are to him. If the answer was, "Not very much," then what was Bancroft doing in Germany? And what was he doing saying all this to the man who had given him a great deal of money and sent him three thousand miles precisely in order to study Horace and Greek metres (among other things)? Partly, Bancroft could say these things because Kirkland wanted to hear them.

Over and over again Bancroft reaffirms the value and authenticity of what the Germans have to offer:

It is wonderful to see how a learned man can look back on antiquity, how intimately he can commune with her, how he rests upon her bosem as upon the bosem of a friend. He can hear the still feeble voice, that comes from the remote ages, and which is lost in the distance to common ears. The darkest portion of history becomes quite transparent when reason and acuteness are united with German perseverance. It is admirable to see with what calmness and patience every author is read, every manuscript collected, every work perused, which can be useful, be it dull or stupid, to see how the most trifling coins and medals, the ruins of art and even the decay of nature is made to bear upon the investigated subject.[57]

Yet, over and over again he denies their worth:

A German man of letters is very different from the idea formed of a scholar in America. Here learning is not ever the companion in public life, nor the beautifier of retirement, nor the help & comforter in affliction, but is attended to as a trade, is cultivated merely because one can get a living by it.[58]

The image of scholarship as a trade was particularly offensive to Kirkland, who had himself often excoriated American culture for its mercantile obsessions. Indeed, he had publicly assailed it as one of the chief barriers to American literary flowering.[59] To patriotic American educators (like Kirkland),[60] whose pedagogical models invariably came from the northern side of the Mediterranean, the image of excessive commercialism still carried the taint of corruption which, unredressed, might well lead to premature decline.[61]

Thus, when young Bancroft repeatedly referred to the German academic system as quintessentially commercial,[62] he was irreparably tainting the whole enterprise. And, despite some contrary testimonials, he continued to do so throughout the time in Germany. Not only did his discovery of the commercial nature of the German academic system appear to disappoint his idealistic hopes for it as a moral as well as intellectual instruction, but it also seemed to tinge the very subjects themselves:

most of them carry on a trade with the labors of the soul, one selling Latin, & another Greek & a third philosophy & a fourth the art of painting. But they are all to be honoured sincerely: for they are capital tradesmen in their respective lines of business.[63]

Bancroft's game with Kirkland had been carried to a ludicrous extreme; it had contaminated the whole enterprise of German learning and virtually insured that Bancroft could learn nothing more in Germany and carry little of what he had learned back with him.[64] He was getting ready to abandon Germany and German scholarship, even as Everett had done.

These two Americans were certainly not alone in their reaction to Germany.[65] Although the evidence is not nearly so extensive, most of the other Americans in this first generation had, in varying degrees, similar experiences.

George Ticknor, whose *Life, Letters and Journals*[66] is the standard source for the experiences of Americans in German universities, appears in those pages to have thoroughly enjoyed his experiences abroad. But even in those perfect, inscribed, and polished entries a contrary feeling comes through. In a passage omitted from the published volumes of the diary, as well as from the extensive excerpts by Orie Long, Ticknor admits:

Today closes my second semestre in Göttingen, and I am grateful to heaven that another period of my imprisonment has passed, for five so miserable months as the last have been have never before darkened my life.[68]

What was it that had made this period of study five "miserable months as . . . have never before darkened my life"? Ticknor is tantalizingly unspecific. He was not homesick, for he was to travel for more than two years between leaving Göttingen and returning to Boston. In a number of places he was to suffer many more inconveniences and setbacks than he had endured in Göttingen without indicating any such feelings.[69] He was neither engaged nor married. He was not buried in hopelessly recondite studies but in comparatively relevant subjects like Modern German and Romance languages, literatures, and history.

Nor was his discontent a result of an isolated bout of depression. Six months later he gave evidence of the same attitude: "Today I have closed the last wearisome semestre of my labours and imprisonment here." And he adds that he looks forward with impatience to his "emancipation."[70] He may simply have been weary of hard intellectual labor, but the suspicion remains that he was at the very least uncomfortable with the new German scholarship. In the end he retained very little German philology, absorbing instead the history of Spanish language and literature, which he studied at Madrid.

Joseph Green Cogswell, the oldest of the first Americans to study in Germany, often appears to have been the most committed. But his commitment was hardly steady and credible. He was often possessed by an overwhelming sense of despair which kept him from any kind of scholarly work. Even when he did manage to overcome it and work hard, this sense of doom often surfaced:

For my own part I am sorry that I came here, because I was too old to be *upset,* like a horseshoe worn thin I shall break as soon as I shall wear in the other side, it makes me very restless at this period of my life, to find that I know nothing; I would not have wished to have made the discovery, unless I could at the same time been allowed to remain in some place where I could get rid of my ignorance.[71]

This was the same lament that Everett had raised, though Cogswell had considerably more justification. When he did manage to overcome the melancholy sense of his own inadequacy, he worked so hard that his health broke down. Was this morbidly self-destructive behavior?[72] The evidence is not quite firm enough to judge. But his sense of anxiety over the distance between what he knew and what the Germans knew was overwhelming. Cogswell fet it more acutely than some of the others, and he was more honest in revealing it:

It has been a mistake to have grasped at too much & now at a period of my life, in which the mind cannot be brought to new talents, to find myself in a situation like that of a privateer under the command of an irresolute captain at sea in the midst of numerous ships, when after successively selecting one and another in the chase, they are at last all making their escape.[73]

It was not only Cogswell who felt himself at sea, however; he was simply less reticent than the others in confessing so to his friends.

Part of the ostensible reason for Bancroft's uneasiness was the threat of apostasy in the German universities. And this also figured largely in the criticisms of Theodore Dwight Woolsey. Yet Woolsey had endured his own crisis of faith long before setting foot in Germany. He assiduously avoided studying theology there. Nevertheless, he was still put on his guard by none other than the indefatigable Moses Stuart:

In the meantime, *to live close to God in your closet* is your only safe-
guard. This will be effectual if you are constant & uniform. I have reason
to believe that your cousin H[enry] D[wight] suffered in his spiritual
state while at Berlin; & if so he became a sufferer through neglect of his
duty. I could predict it without danger of being mistaken.[74]

There was little danger of Woolsey's being led astray. Not only
was he an unusually pious and earnest young man, even for a
Yale graduate, but he cordially detested the enthusiasm and
openness of Henry Dwight's approach. In contrast, Cousin
Woolsey had hardly set foot on the Continent before ringing
denunciations of the Old World were issuing from his pen.
Nor did these cease when he reached Germany.[75]

That it might prove difficult to absorb a great deal from
people whom you constantly derided as moral barbarians
apparently did not occur to Woolsey. Nor did he ever question
the value of his father's rather large outlay to expose Theodore
to these evils. This might be considered a little remarkable in
a man who had already professed a crisis in his own belief and
announced his intention of becoming a specialized scholar
something like the Germans he so tirelessly derided. Woolsey
did more than that, for he announced his intention of becoming
every bit as eminent as the Germans he scorned and of being
employed in the closest thing to a German university the
America of the day had:

Should God give me health I can become in two years of study or professorship a very sound scholar and in five or ten, one to be classed with
the better class of such in Europe. My desire is to be employed in some
college or high literary institution; but nothing would please me so much
as to be engaged in such an institution as you mentioned being talked of
at New York, where my duties would be to lecture to young men rather
than to boys, and to be perfectly free from those little vexations of college
government, which disturb the life of most of our college professors.[76]

The institution referred to was the University of the State of
New York, which at this point existed only as vague talk. In
this early period the chief characteristic of these plans was their
criticism of the traditional American college system and the
hope to have an institution modeled much more closely on the
German system. So Woolsey, in expressing his desire to be
associated with such a university, was explicitly contradict-

ing the views that he had espoused against his cousin, Henry Dwight, whose polemic for the superiority of the German system, as well as his attempts to found a gymnasium in New Haven, Woolsey had buried with derision and contempt.[77]

It was a confusion that was very real and persistent; but it was a dilemma which, unfortunately for Yale, Woolsey never really confronted. On the strength of his own exceedingly inflated claims for his German studies (highly ironic and hypocritical, in light of his real feelings),[78] he was appointed professor of Greek at Yale and sixteen years later, president.

It is difficult to make anything of this morass of contradictions, confusions, proclamations, anxieties, subversions, and doubts. Was it a simple matter of George Bancroft's youth and lack of judgment? Yet the confusions are present in the more sophisticated Everett and Ticknor, as well as in Cogswell and Woolsey. Was it merely the stressful situation? Perhaps. It was certainly painful and distressing to travel thousands of miles across a dangerous ocean to study in a strange land for years on end. A letter could take six weeks or two months to arrive, and many months could go by without even being able to speak to a compatriot.[79] Yet the doubts persisted long after these men returned home. They simply could not come to terms with German scholarship in any consistent and positive way.

Was this solely a theological problem? Did the Americans find it so difficult to come to terms with German study because it seemed to generate infidelity? This must be at least partly true. The issue was certainly important in their minds and in their correspondence. But the theological issue was more than a little suspicious. It appears to have been used by the Americans as a cover for other concerns and fears. There is virtually no sign of a real crisis of faith among any of the first generation of students that has been mentioned. Yet all in some way referred to the moral and intellectual danger posed by German academic scholarship.

It is indeed puzzling that the Americans could have done as some of them said they would: use the benefits of German scholarship for their own ends—use it, for example, for Bancroft's ideal of a truly "republican" learning and culture. That would have been a simple or constructive way out of the dilemma of dealing with the potentially dangerous learning.

As Bancroft says so confidently after a few months' study: "The German rules of criticism are in general right, tho' not unlimitedly right. Their application is sadly wrong, but I feel confident that their laws, their accuracy, & their boldness may be brought to secure a good cause."[80] Why does Bancroft, like all the others, retreat from this apparently simple goal? It is curious that none could use German scholarship for "legitimate" ends. Everett gave the excuse that he was too old and unprepared even to assimilate the German lessons: "Those of us that have hitherto come, have come without preparation, or for too short a time, and in many cases return—when our pilgrimage is over—to our wallowing in the professional mire."[81]

It is true that the Americans were less well-prepared than German students who had attended the best gymnasia such as Schulpforta or Ilfeld. But they seem to have been no worse than most German students; and they were much harder working, by and large, than the Germans. Their principal deficiency, apart from the problem of speaking, understanding, and writing German, seems to have been in using Latin, which was still the language of some lectures and all degree examinations in Germany. But this obstacle was not insurmountable and became less important as Latin declined, and its use became increasingly ceremonial.[82] The Americans' other visible deficiency was their lack of a thorough knowledge of Greek literature and a certain lack of ease in reading the language. But here again the obstacle was far from insurmountable, and in fact most of the Americans seem to have made up their deficiencies rather quickly. On the whole they appear to have been quite exceptional students. Certainly they impressed their instructors as such and were remembered with unusual fondness. For years Eichhorn, Dissen, and Benecke at Göttingen terrified later American arrivals with stories of the prodigious labors and learning of the first of their countrymen to study there.

As for Everett's next excuse—that the Americans stayed too short a time—this was sometimes true. But almost all of them studied for at least two years, and many for three or four. More important, almost no one was forced to curtail his time in Germany. Nearly everyone could have remained longer. Even so, they probably studied as long as most German students, and the latter tended to lose a certain amount of time in social activities in which the Americans did not participate. Even scholars in the philosophical faculty would take their doctorates well within the time that most Americans stayed. George Bancroft got his in just two years.

Everett's last excuse seems to come closer to the point for most Americans. Since college teaching can scarcely be said to have existed as a professional career, only law or the ministry offered any outlet for a humanistic education. Neither of those two professions would offer much scope for the exercising of esoteric German scholarship. But, curiously enough, none of this applied to Everett or his compatriot Ticknor. Both of them had been expressly charged with the task of introducing German scholarship to Harvard. If anyone at all did not have to return home "to wallow in the professional mire," it was these two. Virtually no one had preceded them in Germany. What, then, was the source of Everett's concern that his hard-won German knowledge would prove of little use? He, the holder of the most exciting and academically privileged academic post in America, would have a greater chance than anyone else to apply what he had learned. Where did his anxiety come from?

Part of it, of course, stemmed from Everett's (and Bancroft's, Ticknor's, and Cogswell's) mentor, John Kirkland. Samuel Morison has described Kirkland as "one of the most remarkable presidents that Harvard has ever had, and the best beloved," and he asserts that "until the age of Eliot every successive regime was referred to his as a standard."[83] There is, however, a fundamental problem with Kirkland's service that few Harvard historians discuss. The president who acted so generously and liberally in sending Everett and Bancroft to Germany with large sums of money, and was responsible for hiring them and Ticknor and Cogswell, was also the same president who was responsible for three of them leaving within four years and the fourth serving out his time for another decade until he could go.

Some historians merely desribe Kirkland at each moment of his presidency, without attempting a coherent explanation. Russell Nye speaks of Kirkland in 1817 as "always alert to any means of improvement for his faculty," and proclaims that "Harvard under Kirkland was at the opening of a great period of greatness."[84] But a few years and several pages later, Nye refers to "the stubborn opposition of Kirkland and the Corporation to new ideas."[85] Other historians have caught contradictions in Kirkland's attitude and actions without stopping to ponder what effect these might have had, or of exactly what they might be a sign. Van Wyck Brooks writes:

He was not a man to oppose any important change in the system of studies; and before the end of his long reign, in fact, certain changes were to occur that were eventually to transform the college. But he did not see why the changes should occur. He thought the old ways were good enough, and he played into the hands of firmer men who thought that all other ways were bad.[86]

This certainly gives us a sense of the position in which Kirkland found himself, between the unruly students, the dissatisfied faculty, and the intractable corporation. But it does not explain Kirkland's actions. If the president "did not see why changes should occur," why did he send Everett and Bancroft to Germany? And why did he write them repeatedly not only soliciting their ideas for reform but promising to go the limit in enacting them?

Samuel Morison sees Kirkland as a beleaguered liberal, an astonishing prototype of the beset university presidents of the 1960s:

It was delicate matter to reform Harvard; one that required tact and patience as much as enthusiasm and learning. Cogswell and Bancroft, exasperated with President Kirkland because he did not back them to the limit, lived to admit that Kirkland was probably right. The President wanted reform, and he was determined to resist the popular American demand for a cheap and practical rather than a sound and liberal education. . . . On the other hand he knew that Harvard was too old and sturdy to be pulled up by the roots and replaced by a fresh crop of plants grown from German seed.[87]

This sounds balanced and plausible, but it seriously misrepresents the situation. Far from backing Bancroft and Cogswell to the limit, Kirkland did not back them at all.[88] And if one may venture a surmise to penetrate the thick veil of the corporation meetings, he actively opposed them. The reference to "the fresh crop of plants grown from German seed" is a "natural" completion of the organic metaphor for the college; but it, too, is less than accurate. These seedlings were native–New England planted and Harvard nurtured. Moreover, none of them showed the slightest inclination to deflower New England culture root and branch; nor did they wish to graft the German system whole onto Harvard stock. Morison's easy liberal dogmas are clearly inadequate to explain what is, in psychological terms, a complex situation.

Not just Bancroft or the other American students but Kirkland himself was seriously divided, not just about reform or about German scholarship, but about what higher scholarship was. The dilemma that Kirkland faced was both real and confusing. Yet, within the context of New England values and the Harvard tradition, it could be handled. Transported to the terrifying and alien environment of the German university, the leisured liberality of Kirkland's Harvard could not help confused young graduates. The result was a massive psychic battle.

These young American students were fighting larger cultural battles within their own personal lives. Anxieties which appear to be purely personal for each of them are charged with an extrapersonal meaning. What may seem to a modern eye to be simply career decisions are invested with an ominous Faustian foreboding.

The reasons for these puzzling and intense anxieties are difficult to reconstruct clearly. As we have noted, there are many contributing causes and forces. But at the center of the whole phenomenon is the field of study which enticed the Americans to German universities: philology. To claim that it represented a substitute, secular religion would be inadequate. Its promise of "authentic" knowledge was a religious promise; but it offered as well a rational and methodical approach to the mysteries of language, poetry—and religion.

Clearly, however, the German shamanism of the word was a threatening, even dangerous force within the context of early nineteenth-century America. Fortunately, the philological impulse could be easily transmuted, as it was in Germany, into more socially tractable directions. To both Americans and Germans the idealistic rhetoric of Herder and Humboldt had an immediate and relevant appeal and message, for philology provided an authentic source of national inspiration at a critical moment in history. Bancroft's vision of a philological scholarship that would reveal the ancient texts in their pristine purity and thus furnish the stimulus to national creativity and morality echoes the rhetoric of Humboldt and Herder. Both the Americans and the Germans saw philology as a means of regenerating their countries, to set them on the path to a glorious creativity.

This nationalistic vision of a humanistic scholarship which was to move Germans, Slavs,[89] and Americans in the German universities was not just something in the air at those universities. Not only the political efforts of the German student societies, but the researches and rhetoric of the professors encouraged the link between nationalism and scholarship. It was not just the patriotic efforts of Humboldt, but the seemingly apolitical researches of Ranke, Niebuhr, and other classical as well as national historians and philologists which, just as much as the work of the Grimms, made scholarship into a support for national aspirations. Bancroft's search for a committed and "relevant" scholarship was unusual neither in Germany nor America. His call for a philology that would be politically involved relied specifically on the German example:

Neither is Philology a study fit only for the recluse. It can adorn & give pleasure to the highest. The sciences, which are at first more striking & which are employed in something more tangible are perhaps more cultivated; & belles lettres will perhaps ever find more willing votaries. In America, Philology is a poor forlorn one, who must hide her head in the obscurity of retirement, & may not venture herself beyond the walls that confine her; in Germany she goes out into the high places, into the market & the cities, aye into the courts of kings and emperors, & there finds honours & followers.[90]

Philology in Germany, however, was neither so powerful nor so pure as Bancroft claimed, as he was very soon to discover. It was hardly the guiding light of national destiny and creativity that he sought. No reality could fulfill these ideals. Bancroft pulled back and disassociated himself from the Germans, although he never abandoned his own vision of scholarship. Thus, at the moment when he received his doctorate at Göttingen, he consciously distanced himself from the values and expectations of his German teachers:

So too when the mighty Eichhorn last Saturday ended a congratulatory speech to me with the words, I might live to write a good many books out of the stories I had gathered at Göttingen, I could but smile to see how the πολυγραψος placed the highest enjoyment of life on the πολυγραφια. As if a man could not live very happily & delight in letters without ever dreaming of innundating the world with octavos.[91]

Bancroft obviously had no foreknowledge of the large number of quarto volumes with which he was so quickly to inundate the world.

But these were not to be drawn solely "out of the stores I had gathered at Göttingen"; for his scholarship was not to be that of his German teachers. Vernon Parrington called Bancroft's *History of the United States* "The greatest and in some respects the most characteristic work of the period."[92] Yet Robert Skotheim, assessing the multivolume work, writes, "his treatment of ideas was almost identical with that of his colonial predecessors."[93] The answer to the question why this should be so must go back to his partial rejection of his German experience.

Neither Bancroft's experience nor his rejection is unique. The anxiety of all the others in the first group of Americans is clear and manifest. Most of them pulled back from a complete acceptance of German academic and scholarly values. Though wanting to learn everything, they studied only languages.[94] Though appreciating the work of the most daring and advanced scholarship, they disavowed such endeavors. They saw the German academic system as an alien thing, an alien trade, not just because Kirkland wanted them to, or simply because it was theologically or politically safe to, but because it was psychologically necessary for them to. Having been tempted by it, Americans made the modern form of scholarship as it developed in Germany an alien thing.

CHAPTER 5

The German student reads Homer with the eye of a Grecian, who is familiar with its Society, and with the thoughts and actions of the heroic age. We peruse the Iliad with the views formed solely by the manners and the feelings and systems of the nineteenth century. The former, by his previous studies, has been able to transport himself to a distant age and people. While we, standing at a distance of nearly three thousand years, look with the feelings we have acquired from our peculiar education, at a century which seems infinitely remote.

—Henry Edwin Dwight
Travels in the North of Germany

The Funeral Pyre of Greece:
From the First to the Second Generation
of Americans in German Universities

Henry Dwight's lament for the inadequacy of American scholarship was just and precise. Despite the migration of dozens of able and intelligent American students to German universities and repeated exposure to the new classical scholarship, this scholarship did not survive the return journey to America. Americans continued to interest themselves in classical studies throughout the first half of the nineteenth century. They sent an increasing number of students to the German universities. Their interest in history increased substantially. But the historicist approach of the new classical philology eluded them until the latter half of the nineteenth century. American humanism and American scholarship simply did not drink from the same intellectual spring as the Germans.

Yet a modern form of scholarship in the humanities did emerge in America, and it emerged at a relatively early date, by the last quarter of the nineteenth century. What were the forces which both allowed for the rapid development of the new form of scholarship but blocked the historicistically grounded classical philology for so long?

A large part of the answer can be found in the curious and embattled position of classical studies (embattled much sooner than in Europe) within American education. But that is not the whole story. While internal warfare denied classical philology a legitimate place in American education for so many years, advanced scholarship of the form pioneered by the German classical philologists found increasing favor within the social values of nineteenth-century America.

In his desperate flight from German scholarship, George Bancroft arrived at precisely the point from which the Germans had begun: namely, "the funeral pyre of Greece." In other words, he proclaimed the connection between the literary remains of the glorious ancient republics and the literary and scholarly works of the glorious modern Republic. And when he appealed to his countrymen to light the torch of artistic and literary glory at the Grecian pyre, he was calling for a new use of the classics in American life. This was perhaps the only part of the German vision which he and Everett could bring back to America. Though both of them were to proclaim it vigorously to provincial Boston for several years, both were shortly to abandon it.

In an article in the *North American Review,* Bancroft made explicit the connection between nationalism and classical study. Americans "should find pleasure in being instructed in the 'rules of ancient liberty,' how a people may provide for its prosperity and glory."[1] They should use the classics as allies against the perfidious English and their taste and literature: "The study of the classics deserves, therefore, to be encouraged as a means of preserving national literary independence."[2] The classics would also strengthen the national character by providing a wholesome antidote to the American predilection for utility:

At this epoch, therefore, while the nation is so rapidly forming its character, and while it is still possible to introduce new elements, the study of classical letters deserves to be encouraged, because it tends to awaken and cherish a love for the arts, by which a society is adorned and refined.[3]

Moreover, the classics deserved to be studied because: "In a free country . . . there should be no limits to inquiry," and "it is desirable that the condition of man in every age be known." Finally, Bancroft adds, "the last reason why we should defend the study of classical literature is, that it is the best."[4]

This last sentence is instructive. It was, of course, what Winckelmann, Herder, Heyne, and Humboldt had all believed. But they would not have stated it in those terms. To them, the study of classical literature did not have to be defended. For what they preached was not just the study of classics, but immersion in the spirit of the ancient civilizations. The fire and exuberance of Winckelmann's impassioned conviction seem totally absent in this defense by Bancroft. The spirit of the latter is measured and rational, almost eighteenth-century, by contrast with any German polemic of the previous fifty years. Yet Edward Everett, whose powers as a speaker and writer considerably exceeded those of his younger colleague, had little better success. Though his powerful manner and voice won the hearts of a few Boston ladies and men, most notably Emerson's,[5] they produced little effect. The new American Republic proved less attracted than Frederican Prussia to the glories of the ancient civilizations, the funeral pyre of Greece.

One of the principal reasons for this lack of interest in the new German approach to Greek and Roman culture was that it was obscured totally by the debate on the place of classical study within the college curriculum. Robert Bridges Patton, another Göttingen-trained student who had studied there at the same time as Bancroft, approached this question directly. While his recognition that "the unadaptedness of the present mode to the end at which we profess to aim, its inefficiency in promoting even *literary* culture, and, of course, the necessity of reform,"[6] would seem to place him among the opponents of the classics, such was not the case. In his *Lecture on Classical and National Education* he takes a stand close to that of Bancroft, endorsing the nationalistic value of a sound classical education. But he also demanded a place in the college curriculum for "useful studies demanded by the flourishing condition of our country, and by the enterprise of our citizens."[7] Within the context of the contemporary debate this was an inconsistent position. Patton, however, justified it by calling for a more thorough classical preparation prior to college, the achievement of which would allow for a greater breadth and diversification in the college course. Like so many others, he lamented that:

The studies of our colleges are, as yet, so elementary, so introductory, as it were, to the riper pursuits of after life, that no time can be spared for more extensive and liberal investigations, unsuited at that moment to the capacities and the degree of literary improvement of our college students.[8]

If the preparatory schools could be persuaded to do their job, the proper aim of the college, Patton asserted, would be to foster "research," and he asked for the libraries and other aids that would allow for such a rise in "the standard of literary attainment."[9]

This attempt to have the academies and grammar schools assume a greater responsibility for a basic education in the classics so as to free the colleges for both new subjects and a deeper penetration of its offerings was a hopeful way out of the interminably debated problem of the classical curriculum in the colleges. Unfortunately, it met with no greater success than Bancroft's and Everett's efforts to stir up interest in the new classical scholarship. The infamous Yale report of 1828 took a position directly opposite that of Patton, cheerfully embracing the thankless task of elementary instruction in the classics.[10] Yale demonstrated its concern for the preservation of humanistic education—but at the expense of any kind of change. Humboldt's humanistic vision was clearly beyond the reach of the American imagination. And if the colleges persisted in this defense of preparatory studies, there was little chance of any kind of advanced classical scholarship of the sort to which Patton, Everett, and Bancroft had been exposed.

Thus, the issue of the classical curriculum in the colleges proved to be the tarbaby of American educational reformers and classical teachers alike until the decisive curriculum reforms of Charles Eliot in the 1870s. And the terms in which Bancroft had enunciated the utility of classical learning persisted throughout the same period. They were not fruitful terms, and it is another ironic measure of Bancroft's (among others) resistance to his German training that a German-educated person could have used them at all. All the same, they were intoned faithfully and earnestly by two generations of American classicists. Professor N. F. Moore of Columbia spoke them in his 1835 *Lectures on the Greek Language and Literature.* So spoke the learned professors Sear, Edwards, and Felton in their *Classical Studies: Essays on Ancient Literature and Art* of 1843. So spoke the learned principal of Phillips Andover in 1870. So spoke the dozens of reviews and articles of popular and learned journals in the intervening years. And virtually every opponent of the Bancroft views argued within those terms. The tarbaby stuck.

Every attempt to break out of the sterile molds of utility,

by both reformers and classicists, failed. President Quincy of
Harvard tried valiantly to raise the standard of classical studies
within the university by every means short of modifying the
curriculum. But his belated admission that this last measure,
too, was necessary, was greeted with intolerant skepticism. In
vain he protested the necessity of his proposals:

The end proposed by the Resolutions is to introduce into the University
such a system of studies, as may enable the Corporation to establish a real
standard in the Greek and Roman languages, and to remove the obstacles,
which under the present system now prevent the institution from raising
it to its greatest practical height.[11]

Quincy understood all too well Patton's contention that the
elementary nature of the college curriculum constituted the
greatest impediment to the advancement of classical scholarship
itself:

the effect acts directly and powerfully upon the state of classic scholarship in the University. It is a material obstacle to the higher elevation of
classical attainment, even by the humble method of increasing the number
of books, or the amount of time to be expended on these branches. For
every increase of this kind is an increase in the obnoxious requisitions
of the Institution, and disgusts and deters more from partaking of its
privileges.[12]

But the president's arguments disgusted and deterred his critics
even more than his previous reforms had done. And if there was
a large class in the community who regarded "such studies as a
waste of time and labour,"[13] there was an equally large and
even more important group (whose "patronage" was even more
"essential to the support of the College") who considered the
studies sacrosanct. Neither was pleased with what both regarded
as Quincy's double talk on the subject of standards of classical
scholarship:

Those who apprehend that this project will effect a reduction in the standard of classical literature, mistake both the intention and the effect. No
real standard of classical attainment has been, or is established at Harvard,
nor, so far as is known, in any college in this country; and so long as the
present system of studies is pursued never can be.[14]

By "standard" Quincy meant specifically a "thorough,
searching, individual examination" that would be made "the

criterion of a degree."[15] He argued that such an examination was impossible within the old curriculum, since it would inevitably "deprive the seminary of one third, if not one half of the graduating class; and give offence to the most important portion of the community."[16] But Quincy's critics regarded this as unabashed sophistry. The tarbaby continued to stick. The conundrum of the classical curriculum proved to be an insurmountable barrier to the introduction of the new form of classical scholarship in the colleges and universities.

Notwithstanding the attacks on the classical curriculum and the laments of its defenders that it was even then being subverted, virtually everyone agreed that the level of classical learning both inside and outside the classroom had risen significantly from the previous generation. An 1842 notice from the *North American Review* began:

One cannot help being struck, in looking over the pages of this book [C. C. Felton's Greek Reader], with the difference in standards of American scholarship now, and in the days removed from us by only one generation.[17]

The fact that he was reviewing a mere school reader and not an advanced work of classical scholarship did not restrain the reviewer from equating it with the latest and best European work. The truth was that no comparison was yet possible: the Americans were still working at a different level.[18] True, Quincy himself had raised the standard at Harvard by demanding more classical knowledge on the entrance exam, establishing the infamous "Scale of Merit," and hiring some more German-trained professors. But his 1841 *Remarks* was a confession of the limits of such a policy. Harvard's enrollment had declined drastically as a direct result of these actions; and within that circumstance nothing that would further alienate powerful and essential support could be accomplished.

Yet even outside Harvard the appeal for a new kind of classical scholarship went no further. Cornelius Felton, Harvard's German-trained successor to Everett in the Eliot Professorship of Greek, was too loaded down with elementary recitations and a restrictive syllabus to do more than churn out school editions and readers. Theodore Woolsey, his counterpart at Yale, operated under the same handicap and produced the same kind of work. If these two German-trained scholars, the fore-most American classicists of their day at the two leading univer-sities, could not (or would not) practice the new German scholarship, there was no one else who could or would. Vir-tually every other college teacher of Greek and Latin operated under even greater handicaps than these two. It is symptomatic of the low state of classical studies in the United States that as late as 1847 such an established journal as *The Knickerbocker* would rely on the pontificating, newly graduated Charles Astor Bristed to review the work of the Eliot Professor of Greek at Harvard. It is even more symptomatic that at least some of his obnoxiously worded criticisms were correct.[19] The American college and university of the period were simply inadequate as matrixes of the new scholarship. The revolution in scholarship in the humanities which in Germany had begun with a general and widespread enthusiasm for classical art and literature and the reform of school teaching based on a new understanding of classical culture could not and did not proceed from the same intellectual or social matrix in America.

But that does not mean that philology and advanced scholar-ship were not possible without that kind of origin. Classical philology was not only possible in America, it did in fact de-velop. But it did not emerge until the last half of the nineteenth century, along with opportunities for advanced scholarly work in the new universities and the specialized journals and profes-sional societies. In other words, it developed around the same time as most of the other scholarly disciplines in the humani-ties, and not, as in Germany, before them. And these other disciplines did not in America, as they had in Germany, take their paradigms from classical philology.

Simply for these reasons we might well expect that the form and development of classical scholarship differed greatly in America. And this is substantially true. American philology lacked that evangelical fervor, that sense of transcendent purpose which informed German scholarship in so many ways even after belief in it had withered. This older German concep-tion had clearly subordinated the impulse for specialization to the higher goal of *Neuhumanismus,* which one might translate in this context as the imperative for a sympathetic understand-ing of the creativity of man and men in historical cultures. The philological scholarship that developed a century later in America was more rigidly specialized not only because of its late emergence but also because of its more social, rather than ideological, matrix.

It is hardly surprising that the American matrix was indisputably elitist throughout the first half-century of the student migration to Germany. John Adams is one of the first witnesses to that fact in a letter of reference he wrote to Thomas Jefferson:

Mr. Everett is respectable in every view: in Family Fortune Station Genius Learning and Character. What more ought to be said to Thomas Jefferson by

John Adams[20]

What crusty old John Adams said in 1814 was to be repeated for a very large number of American students who journeyed to the German universities. A half-century later another letter of reference read:

Mr. Smith, like myself, is from Delaware County, Pennsylvania and is the son of Dr. George Smith, one of the most prominent and influential citizens of this State.[21]

The suspicion that sons of "prominent and influential citizens" and those "respectable in every view"—especially that of Family Fortune—constituted the largest number of those students in the years between the two quoted letters cannot be proved. Yet, even if they did not actually make up the majority, the fact remains that the American elite were far from loath not only to send their sons to Europe for several years following college, but to have them engaged in hard scholarly effort in a German university. Thus it is hardly surprising that by the time many American colleges and universities had become permeated with a large number of German-trained scholars, the social elite of Boston was similarly infiltrated.

The growing status of German study did not depend solely on the sons of the elite, however. Marriage and association played a large part in the social legitimization of scholarship. Men respectable in every view but that of Family Fortune, Longfellow for example, were easily able to make marriages that went a long way toward endowing an intellectual elite with status as well as money. Others, like the legendary Samuel Ward, made (and in Ward's case, lost) their own fortunes, mingling with both the intellectually and socially powerful in the process. Samuel Eliot, whose father had anonymously endowed the chair which Everett first assumed at Harvard, stopped for several months in Berlin and Göttingen. He experienced a sense of heartfelt revulsion toward Göttingen professors.[22] But he continued to associate with a long list of others who made the journey, including his own son. Andrews Norton rather evidently overreacted to Bancroft's European ways. But he, too, continued to associate with the men who made the trek to Göttingen, as did his son, though neither of them ever studied there. Through visible and invisible social interaction, the idea of German scholarship gradually acquired a respectability and status in America that it never quite attained in either France or England.

When the cost of traveling to Germany dropped after the introduction of transatlantic steamer service and railroads, it became much easier for families of considerably less means to send their sons to German universities. The two Whitney brothers could satisfy their untranscendental longings for real German instruction as they might not have done before. By the 1860s even poor boys like G. Stanley Hall could earn or borrow enough for the trip over. Yet, even through the 1860s the sons of the elite continued to migrate in large numbers.

This is not to say that study in the German universities had become simply another form of the Grand Tour. Americans with inclinations of that sort did not have to subject themselves to the rigor of the German university.[23] They usually managed to confine themselves to more traditional Grand Tour activities in London, Paris, Florence, and Rome. For all the vaunted freedom of the German universities, they could not compare with the unfettered existences of the large cosmopolitan cities. The small provincial towns in which most of them were set could not compete with Paris or Rome. Even Berlin was not in the same league. *Lernfreiheit* never implied any other freedom.

For someone like John Lathrop Motley, for example, the hard years at Göttingen and Berlin could hardly be called a Grand Tour. This son of a wealthy Boston merchant studied hard under Savigny. Yet his motivation could hardly be called scholarly or professional. Though he was later to complete a monumental history, *The Rise of the Dutch Republic,* he did not follow an academic career. Later secretary of the American Mission at St. Petersburg and then minister to Austria, his first choice was literary work and his first published book a novel, *Morton's Hope* (one of the few sources for Bismarck's early life).[24] Thus, one of the most sophisticated and specialized historians of his day, despite his advanced training in the German universities, did not follow a "professional" career. Or, to put it another way, a course of study and training which was very soon to become almost exclusively professional or vocational was not used that way by Motley. And the same is true of a large number of the early students in Germany.

Although George Ticknor did teach modern languages at Harvard for fifteen years, the rest of his life was not at all devoted to teaching. Everett only spent a few years as a teacher before running for Congress. He was later governor of Massachusetts and secretary of state. Bancroft, on whom the Harvard Corporation had spent so much money, left the college after a year to found the Round Hill School. He, too, turned to a political career, rising to the positions of secretary of the Navy under Polk, and later serving as the Minister to Berlin. Joseph Green Cogswell also served only a short time as the librarian at Harvard and never returned to a college. Although there were professors like Cornelius Felton, Edward Salisbury, Theodore Woolsey, and Henry Longfellow who came back from their German study and went straight into academic careers, they were not numerous until the 1850s. In fact, that list of four virtually exhausts their number. And Longfellow and Salisbury abandoned their academic careers as soon as they could.

Far more typical in the 1820s, 1830s, and 1840s were students like George Henry Calvert, who graduated from Harvard in 1823 and studied in Göttingen the following year. A poet and essayist, he became editor of the *Baltimore American* and mayor of Newport, Rhode Island, about the time that it became a fashionable resort. Though he was never to do any serious academic research, he lent respectability to German study and tried his hand at some minor translating. His classmate, William Amory, the son of a wealthy Boston merchant, likewise never used his two years at Göttingen and Berlin for serious academic work. But he took a prominent part in Boston and Harvard affairs for a half-century afterwards, and was finally elected a Harvard overseer in 1877.

Virtually the only American student of the humanities in German universities in the 1830s to go on to an academic career was Edward Salisbury. And this trend continued into the 1840s. James Eliot Cabot and John Weiss were typical American students of the humanities in the early 1840s. Weiss had graduated from Harvard in 1837 and registered as a philological student at Heidelberg in 1840. Despite that fact, he went back to Watertown, Massachusetts, as a Unitarian minister. Like Bayard Taylor, who followed him to Heidelberg in 1844, he was a vehement Abolitionist, in fact, so much so that he lost his congregation and had a difficult job finding another one. He retained his interest in German literature and scholarship, however, and was the author of many translations, notably of Schiller.

James Eliot Cabot, who studied in Berlin and Göttingen in the same years as Weiss was in Heidelberg, had graduated from Harvard in 1840. Yet, despite three years of advanced study, he too did not follow an academic career, turning instead to journalism. Like Weiss, he became involved with the Transcendentalist movement and was the author of *A Memoir of Ralph Waldo Emerson.* And, like Amory, he remained active in Harvard affairs, serving as an overseer from 1875 to 1883.

The brilliant young Charles Stearns Wheeler had divided the five years following his graduation in 1837 between Brook Farm and Harvard Square. He was both a tutor at Harvard and a collaborator with Emerson in editing the works of Carlyle. Though he was to die in Leipzig less than two years after beginning German study, he was clearly marked for a scholarly career, having begun an edition of Herodotus for which even his German professors offered their admiration.[25]

Bayard Taylor, who followed him to Leipzig in 1844, lacked Wheeler's scholarly intensity. But in the midst of a stunning career as a journalist, traveler, and minister to Germany, he managed a stretch as a professor of German literature at Cornell from 1870 to 1877. And, having married the daughter of a professor at Erfurt, he kept his German intact with a large number of literary translations.

At the same time when Taylor registered at Dresden and Leipzig, two other Harvard graduates zealously dedicated themselves to the cause of scholarship. "I want the equal development of all my faculties, the realization of the true, the good, and the beautiful; and for this I am ready to give my whole life if necessary," declared George Cabot Ward to Peter August Porter in a Heidelberg attic. "But I desire no results that are not based on solid and real knowledge," he swore.

My call has not come; I must bide my time; I can wait but I cannot give myself for the sake of occupation of success to that which my heart does not tell me I am fitted for. I am conscious of the possession of all my faculties in their prime. Whatever I could have become I still could be; but I cannot choose, I must be chosen.[26]

Evidently classical philology beckoned neither Ward nor Porter to their *Berufs*. Both settled in New York. Ward became a businessman. Porter served as a member of the New York legislature and died relatively young in the Civil War.

If most of the students who went to Germany to study the humanities in the first half of the nineteenth century could not have had any clear-cut professional motivation, if there was no simple vocational preparation, if there were not great numbers of academic posts, that is not to say there was no outlet for the type of knowledge and training they brought back. For there was a developing market for advanced knowledge in the humanities. That it was not and could not hope to be large enough to provide a decent living for all the people with this kind of education is incontrovertible. Nevertheless, for people with some independent means (a large proportion of these students), or for those content to rely on some more lowly trade to earn most of their living, there were increasing opportunities to utilize a more advanced education in the humanities than could be gotten in an American college of the period. These opportunities lay primarily within the emerging literary culture and the numerous small- and medium-sized periodicals which it supported.

At the time when James Russell Lowell began making his career in this market in the 1840s, it could be fairly said that no other poet or critic could have supported himself in this way.[27] Yet with only the smallest supplementary income, he managed to scrape through.[28] He wrote for the prestigious intellectual journals and for the mass-circulation women's magazines. He wrote about Chaucer and Dante and the German poets. And there were others who made their living by writing about even more esoteric subjects, like the latest German monographs. The *North American Review* had started noticing specialized works by German scholars as early as the 1830s. Hermann, Ritter, Boeckh, Buttmann, Niebuhr, and others were made familiar to its readers. Though some of the reviews were embarrassingly late (Wolf's *Prolegomena* had to wait forty years before it was noticed), others were reasonably prompt, often much faster than book reviews today. For reviews of these types of books specialized knowledge was a necessity.

The emerging literary culture of the middle of the nineteenth century provided a growing and increasingly sophisticated market for this kind of knowledge and for a literary-scholarly career. As the periodical- and book-buying public became more cosmopolitan, as their hunger for continental literature and literary tastes grew, so the demand for informed literary criticism and advanced knowledge of medieval and modern European literature and history grew. The demand for this kind of knowledge could not be met by the American colleges of the period and would not be met by American universities until decades later. Part of it was met by those returning from the German universities.

This small but growing literary marketplace not only provided a social and intellectual context for the assimilation (however partial) of the German learning, it also provided additional support for an idea of higher learning and expertise in the humanities. Although the literary culture was essentially "amateur," it assumed throughout this period a perceptibly mediatory role. That is, it increasingly recognized the existence of more specialized and complete knowledge to which access was restricted to professionals. Thus, if a popular journal wanted an article on medieval ballads or classical sculpture, it either had to rely on an expert like J. R. Lowell to give some part of his knowledge, or at least employ someone who had some idea of what the scholars had said. The literary culture, if it could not by itself create the vocation of scholarship, could at least contribute to it, both by employing those with specialized knowledge in the humanities and by increasing the social legitimacy of such a knowledge.

By the end of the 1840s, however, a new spirit was clearly in the offing. Within a period of the last two years of the decade, a new generation of American students began registering in the German universities. This generation would be the first to bring back some part of German scholarship, make advanced academic study a recognized professional vocation, construct and staff the new American universities, and fashion the modern form of scholarship in the humanities in America. In those two years, such men as Francis Child and George Lane, who were to form the backbone of the German-trained faculty at Harvard, Basil Gildersleeve, the first philologist at Johns Hopkins, and William Dwight Whitney, the eminent Yale Sanskrit philologist, studied in Germany. They were joined within five years by such people as Justin Winsor, William Goodwin, and James Russell Lowell, three more of the German-taught contingent at Harvard; Lewis Packard and Daniel Cody Eaton to join Thacher, Salisbury, Woolsey, and Whitney at Yale; and a dazzling array of future college and university presidents, many of whom would be instrumental in creating the modern university in America: James Burrill Angell of the University of Michigan, Andrew Dickson White of Cornell, and the most famous, Daniel Coit Gilman, the builder of Johns Hopkins, as well as the two Seelye brothers, Julius and Lawrence, presidents of Amherst and Smith respectively.

Thus, the five or six years at mid-century witnessed not only the appearance of the largest group of future leaders and pioneers of the American universities, but also the sudden adoption of a standard professional career pattern for advanced scholarship in the humanities. Besides all of the well-known names mentioned above, there were dozens of more obscure students who brought their German experiences to colleges and universities all over the country. Joseph Coolidge Shaw graduated from Harvard, studied at Göttingen and Berlin, converted to Catholicism, joined the Jesuits, and ended up teaching at St. John's and Fordham. William Wells came from Williams to Berlin and went to Genesee and then to Union College. Henry Lorenzo Low started at Dartmouth, studied philology at Berlin, and became a professor at Hobart. Duncan Campbell went from Berlin to Georgetown. William Francis Allen, after some years as a high school teacher, made better use of his advanced historical training in Berlin and Göttingen at Antioch and the University of Wisconsin. He is credited with being a pioneer in the introduction of primary source materials to his history seminars.

Charles Eliot's reform of the curriculum at Harvard in the 1870s and his promotion of graduate studies there are commonly taken as major signs of the emergence of the modern university system in the United States. By that date there were at least nine professors of humanities out of the total Harvard College faculty of twenty-three who had received advanced training in Germany. They had been influential in choosing Eliot (who had himself studied chemistry in Germany) as president. A few weeks before Eliot's final elevation (after a long struggle)[29] to the presidency of Harvard, Francis Child wrote to his friend Francis Parkman, lobbying for his support of Eliot among the overseers and the corporation:

My dear Parkman,

I want only to say that I myself thoroughly approve of Eliot; that I think him a good man for the place, and what is more to the purpose, the best man we can get.

Eliot is a man of clear mind, of active habits, moderate in his views of the relative claims of science and literature, and, what Peabody [Andrew P. Peabody, the acting president] is not, a good judge of men. We especially need a President who will know how to fill vacancies in the faculty.

Do go to the meeting.[30]

Although Eliot was far from the pawn of his German-trained faculty, it is important to note the support that the most influential among them gave him at this critical moment. Child's judgment that Eliot would be the kind of president "who will know how to fill vacancies in the faculty" was exactly prophetic. The German contingent at Harvard was assured that the values which they had acquired would be strengthened by the future appointments at Harvard.

By 1870 Yale also had a half-dozen German-trained professors of the humanities on its faculty, including both the outgoing president Woolsey and the new president Noah Porter. Neither would change Yale into a modern university. But the presence of that number of men with German training would gradually refashion it. By 1870 dozens of American students trained in the humanities in German universities had infiltrated colleges and universities throughout the country. They were to form the advance gaurd of a new kind of institution and a new type of scholarship.

The first generation of Americans in the German universities had great difficulty in assimilating German scholarship in the humanities. Ironically, German higher criticism, despite religious obstacles, found more practitioners and a readier acceptance in America than the new classical philology.[31] America sent hundreds of students to the German universities before 1850. Virtually none of them managed to absorb the new classical philology. Even if they had, the debate over the classical curriculum would have prevented them from passing on their knowledge within the old-time American colleges.

Yet resistance to the new form of classical study did not hinder the assimilation of a generation of American students who had studied in Germany. If they could not follow the vocational channels which led in later decades to a career in academic scholarship, they could aid the gradual acceptance of the legitimacy of higher scholarship. The results of this acceptance were rapid and far-reaching. Within a half-dozen years a career pattern of advanced study in the humanities began to emerge and a large number of the individual pioneers of American higher education were studying in German universities. The psychological and social blocks to advanced scholarship in the humanities appear to have disappeared. Was the experience of German study different for this second generation?

CHAPTER 6

I am sick of Banking & want to take a hold of something that I can put my whole spirit into.
> —William Dwight Whitney to Eliza Whitney,
> February 20, 1849

By George I am getting to be so learned that there is no Spirit left in me. I am all in all given to Philology. Do you know what it is to be a Philologist? Do you suppose that it is a parasitic Weed (Philology) unsightly to the Eye and without Nourishment power? Philology is no Weed, it is if I may use the Expression a spreading Tree, rooted in the human Heart, developing its uneven tall Branches in the Groundsoil of the theoretical. . . . [illegible] its Fruittruths are the only genuine Inhabitants of the Daseyn-realm, its Method is not legitimately historisch-antiquarian, or bibliographic-critic but aesthetic-literary, its Nourishment is drawn from the Willfountains which circulate in the Veins of the psychologic & ontologic Spheres while cum grano salis the Philologist sits perched on the top of the Tree linked to the Body of Literature by an uncut Navel-cord if I may use the Expression and mere common men feed on the Crumbs that fall from him. The last sentence to be frank is none of mine but is taken from Hermann's lecture. I enjoy the lectures very much. . . .
> —Francis Child to C. A. Joy,
> Göttingen, November 1, 1850

I was fortunate to find here [five] of my countrymen by whose assistance I soon became domesticated, & almost forgot that I was in a land of Strangers.
> —Henry E. Dwight to A. Hillhouse,
> September 15, 1825

The "Fruittruths" of Philology:
The Second Generation of
American Students in the German Universities

In 1836, twenty-one years after Everett and Ticknor had first set foot in Göttingen to try their hands at classical philology, another Bostonian came to Germany to study Sanskrit and Arabic. Like Woolsey in 1827 he began his studies in Paris. Unlike Woolsey he continued them at Bonn and Berlin. His name was Edward Elbridge Salisbury, son of a Boston clergyman. He had attended Boston Latin School and Yale College, graduating when his future brother-in-law, Woolsey, was professor of Greek, but before the latter had been elevated to president. Salisbury stayed five years in Europe, working harder than his brother-in-law had done. When he returned in 1841, he became the first professor of Arabic and Sanskrit in the United States, the founder of the American Oriental Society in 1842, and the editor of its journal. Despite these activities, however, Salisbury knew his weaknesses and limitations. He sustained Sanskrit and Indo-European philology at a time when no one else in the United States knew anything of the subject, devoting years and substantial amounts of money to the cause. But he knew that he was not a scholar of the subject to compare with those in Berlin, Tübingen, and Paris. And for eight years he taught virtually no students.

In the fall of 1849, however, a most unusual and advanced student came to New Haven to work with Salisbury, a young man of twenty-two. He had already been hard at work learning Sanskrit. And within five years he was to become the first American really proficient in that language, and the first American philologist whose work could rank with that of the Europeans.

William Dwight Whitney, the second oldest of Josiah Whitney's sons, besides being the most intellectual, was also the most steadfast of the Whitney children. The latter quality was one that counted for a great deal with the elder Mr. Whitney, a merchant and banker of Northhampton, Massachusetts. Nevertheless, William, though he had given the most tangible evidence of his intellectual gifts by entering college at the age of fifteen and graduating three years later at the top of his class at Williams, was to spend the subsequent four years under his father's eye in a Northampton bank. And despite the fact that he soon came to resent the years he had lost to scholarship and yearn for the dingy recesses of a Berlin library, he does not appear to have been greatly out of his element.

The long, meticulously neat columns of figures and notations progressing to precise and unarguable conclusions were in many ways emblematic of W. D. Whitney's personality. These careful accounts were replicated in the long lists of geological and botanical observations that he had begun compiling for himself in college and the exact observations of the daily weather that he was to note every day in his diaries for fifty years. On the weekdays he labored over the bank's account books and on the weekends he added to the long lists of birds sighted, birds shot, and birds stuffed and mounted. For he was as cool and precise a marksman as he was an accountant. And his skill at stuffing and mounting his specimens rivaled the best professionals of the day. Naturally, every specimen was neatly catalogued and mounted in his own well-built bird cases, catalogued in the same neat and unadorned handwriting in which even then he had started the innumerable declensions and grammatical forms of Old Norse, modern Swedish and German, and—ancient Sanskrit.[1] Nearly half a century later the same handwriting enumerates the meticulous account books and membership lists of the American Oriental Society and the American Philological Association.

Josiah Whitney, Jr., in the considered opinion of his father, lacked the qualities of judgment and systematic application of his younger brother William. Nevertheless, at the time when William was slaving away at the bank and his hobbies, Josiah was studying chemistry and geology in Germany and sending enthusiastic letters home to his younger brother. Six months after William had begun his employment Josiah wrote:

You do not tell me how you like the bank, or what your plans are about continuing there. It seems that you have quite given up the idea of studying medicine. I want you to tell me just what your wishes and what you think that Father's wishes and expectations are in this important matter. Of course my first object will be as soon as I return to do all I can to have you enjoy any advantages you may wish in carrying out your education. If, as you propose, you wish to devote your life to the study of Philology and take a Professorship, you must come out here and remain at least three years.[2]

William wrote back saying that he was not entirely happy with the bank, and with the wry humor which made him so beloved by his family and friends he added:

It [the red-headed woodpecker] is moreover getting to be rare & valuable, for the Ornithologists say that it is fast disappearing from the country. The question naturally asserts itself whether this is not a plain intimation, a palpable hint, so to speak, that it is my duty also "to leave my country for my country's good" & bring (fling?) myself for a time at least in the depths of a Berlin library.[3]

Whether his father had made known his "wishes and expectations" to the contrary or whether William, for all his protestations, was for the time being happy enough where he was, is impossible to say. But the correspondence with his brother continued in this vein for a long time, three years to be exact.

Two years after the first letter William wrote: "I cannot tolerate the idea of spending my days at this Bank. I want to go over the puddle as early as next Spring, at the farthest & spend about three years grubbing away at Philology."[4] It was to be yet another two years after that before William was to succeed in "going over the puddle." In the meantime his brother had come home and been sent out on a U.S. Geological Survey to the upper Michigan peninsula. The next summer (1849) William finally quit the bank for three months of backpacking. Typically, he not only brought along his Sanskrit grammar, he studied it.

When he returned to the East he neither went to the bank nor to Germany, but to New Haven, where he commenced to study with the only professor of Sanskrit in the United States, E. E. Salisbury. He had come to make himself into a philologist, though he had only the vaguest conception of what that was. He was as much in doubt, too, of his own abilities and commitment:

> What I wish to study is Comparative Philology generally, which you know, is not the science of languages only, but of language. At present I hardly know more than that it is a most vast important and interesting field; so vast that I am ready to distrust my own senses in respect to their justifying me in devoting myself to labor in it. I know only that at present I am entirely ignorant, & that I have never really *studied;* all that has ever looked like that has been merely rambling & desultory satisfaction of an unenlightened curiosity. Now I am going to try to begin doing something, & I hope I shall succeed, if application will ensure success.[5]

Even before he had begun his studies in New Haven, let alone Germany, and even before he committed himself fully to them, Whitney recognized with precocious clarity the difference between "real study" and "rambling & desultory satisfaction of an unenlightened curiosity," and resolved that if he would become an academic philologist, he would have to do the former. There appears to have been not the slightest possibility of using comparative philology in an amateur way. His father certainly was not prepared to support that. The Whitney frame of mind was unabashedly vocational. And when William picked his study, he picked his vocation. He had not thought of using his studies in something like a theological career. Whitney knew from the beginning that philology was specialized and "vast" and that it required "real study" for itself. And knowing that, he knew much more than most of the Americans who preceded him to Germany.

In the coming months Whitney did not acquire a great deal of advanced knowledge in either Sanskrit or comparative philology. But he did arrive at an increasingly concrete and sophisticated conception of just what philology was and what he needed to know. Commenting on his work on Sanskrit and Greek inflections and the evolution of gutterals from Anglo-Saxon to English, he wrote to his friend Freeman Bumsted:

Stupid stuff too you might perhaps call it, yet after all I would be willing

to leave up to fair & impartial judges whether it were not quite as edify-
ing as a minute dissertation on the stern-hydro-phfnglo muscle, or on the
diseases of teeth, or on the important analogies between the two structures
of porens & homos, & the like, which you are thinking of paramount
interest. Your employment & mine are not so diverse after all; you are
anatomizing & dissecting & studying the disorders & misuses of that which
is the incorporation and container of human life, & I am trying to do the
same thing for that which is the container of human thought: those are my
striking anlogies between body & language in this light, which I leave you
to follow in your leisure.[6]

This lofty conception of the worth of philological scholarship
was not unique among prospective American students of the
subject. What was different about Whitney was not only that
he realized the importance of the "years grubbing away" for
learning a specialized discipline but that he had a clear comprehension of exactly where his long lists of Sanskrit declensions
fitted into this idea. And this comprehension led directly to an
increased confidence:

But I think you would be surprised to learn what wonders have been
accomplished in the investigation of *language* within the past half century,
& how near comparative Philology has come to a complete analysis there-
of, & to turning back the vast & complicated body of languages as they at
present exist to a few simple principles working among & upon a few
simple utterances; & of what essential, even indispensible service the Sanskrit has been in this work. In comparison with it no other language is
worth wasting time upon. I am growing every day to appreciate the high
character of the employment I am engaged in & to feel more enthusiasm
for it, & of course greater pleasure in it.[7]

The search for "a few simple principles" that would make completely intelligible the babble of the earth proved illusory. But
Whitney's conception of the indispensible nature of the Sanskrit
was precocious and accurate. New Haven, in the person of the
shy and intellectually unpretentious Salisbury, had little more
to teach him, and he at last "jumped the puddle" and began his
grubbing in the infamous Berlin library.

The process by which Whitney had arrived at his decision to
make himself into a philologist and study in Germany is mostly
hidden from the historian. But it appears to have been cautious
and deliberate. Perhaps more than any other American who had
gone before, he knew what he wanted and how and where he

was going to find it. If he had no surprises, he also had few illusions. He knew that years of specialized labor awaited him, and the result of this probably would not energize or revolutionize American life or letters. His liminal moments had come and gone; what remained were long years of study.

If Whitney had been more cautious and deliberate about committing himself to a life of academic study and a new kind of scholarship than Bancroft, Everett, or most of the other early American students, it was not simply because he was more phlegmatic than they. He knew more about what was involved in the discipline of comparative philology and what would be its probable future, although he also took a great deal on faith:

Within not many years past, owing chiefly to the introduction of Sanskrit to the knowledge of European scholars, an entirely new province of study, and one of the highest importance, that of comparative philology, has been opened to the world. In consequence of it, as great a revolution has been effected in the study of language & of languages as has been effected in the departments of science. The old systems & methods are being superceded & discarded, & everything is assuming new forms. As yet it has received but little attention in this country, the old men are too old for it; but it must inevitably be introduced & occupy as high a position as any other branch of study in the requirements of American scholarship & the task of accomplishing this is committed to the rising generation. I do not know that to you all this means anything, but I hardly understand how I shall carry to you my convictions of the high & general importance of this study, its inevitable rise & extension in this country, & the certainty that anyone who takes hold of it will be carried up with it, if he does not himself lack the talent which should ensure him success.[8]

This was real Victorian optimism, seemingly as exuberant as the first innocent excitement of the previous generation of American students in Germany. Whitney at this time, unlike Ticknor, Everett, Longfellow, and numbers of others, had no prospects for a professorship. And unlike Bancroft, Woolsey, and others, he did not have the kind of immediately powerful social connections that made employment next to automatic. Partly, his rhetoric is bravado assumed for the expectations and values of his father. Nevertheless, he possessed an authority and conviction that many of the other students with an assured future did not have.

Like his father, pulling money out of the safe and profitable

New England railway stocks and putting it into land and rail-road shares in Ohio in 1851, young Whitney had a sure eye for the coming thing, the safe speculation. The tone of the Victorian entrepreneur, so absolutely appropriate in a letter to his conservative but speculating father, is not an assumed role for Whitney. His faith in the inevitability of the coming historical moment, of the ineluctable progress of scholarship, as well as the indispensability of Sanskrit to that progress, imparted a sense of security absolutely vital for the new type of scholar-ship, the preparation for which could last for many years. The cost of the voyage to Germany and of spending so much time there was now low enough to allow Americans of even middle-class means to study there. The chief barrier was not monetary[9] but psychological: how to sustain an unheard-of level of com-mitment to a new and not yet established profession for so long a period. At a time when college enrollments had already begun drastically to decline relative to the population, this was a real problem. Whitney's serene assurance was essential.

And his faith was more than equal to the demands that were to be placed upon it. His is the Calvinist's confidence in the righteousness of Providence and the triumph of the faithful servant of the Lord. As he wrote to his father:

As to that which I know you feel most solicitous about, whether I shall be able to support myself comfortably & honorably by my profession when obtained, I cannot cherish any doubts on that score. I have entire confidence in the growing appreciation of philology & am sure that I shall receive all the patronage & support of which I show myself deserving.[10]

Since at the time there was no profession such as he took for granted and not a single paid professor of Sanskrit, Whitney was exhibiting more than confidence. This was surely the Protestant ethic and the spirit of capitalism applied to the new territory of scholarship in the humanities. The Horatio Alger tone of the last sentence is reinforced by the following line in the letter: "It may be some time before I am ready to do any-thing more than just live along, but I shall be ready & willing to incounter much that is unpleasant & distressing supported by the hope of what is better, & by the satisfaction & pleasure which I derive from the study itself."[11]

It is much easier to be virtuous when virtue for its own sake is inevitably rewarded. Despite the very real pleasure which Whitney did derive from his studies, however, he did not linger over this point (in a letter greatly given to lingering over the preceding points) and concluded by reiterating the Alger theme: "I should expect when I come home to be above no honorable means of obtaining a livelihood; to begin in a small way, & work gradually up to whatever situation I could."[12] It is not recorded that Whitney ever had to drive a taxi. The Calvinist virtues that had sustained him throughout the four years at the Northampton bank indeed led him on to academic success. In a way he just changed banks.

Yet the Whitney spirit did not allow him to become complacent. The daily psychological pressures of tedious work and prolonged residence in a strange land were as difficult for him as for the earlier Americans. He remarks rather glumly to his diary on the occasion of his birthday:

Twenty four years old today, & on the whole rather ashamed of myself that at so advanced an age, I know so little. Have done nothing in the sentimental line, have not said a word about it to anyone, & have made no new resolutions. That is hardly necessary as my general state of mind is a constant resolution to do the best I can.[13]

Not only was Whitney's state of mind a constant resolution, but he had also been working extremely hard and living as abstemiously as possible. Birthdays, whether personal or national, were anxiety-laden occasions for Americans abroad. But this grim determination and self-criticism were not unusual for Whitney. His vigilant superego precluded self-congratulation:

You are not very far from the truth when you guess that I am tolerably happy here, tho' not so high up in the air as you seem to think. The first point is what a man is, & it is only the second or third point where he is. If I could get into a state of satisfaction with myself & think I was accomplishing all I ought to desire, you might search long for a happier individual, but that is far enough from being the case. I get rather blue sometimes & am always kept in a state of wholesome humility.[14]

Jonathan Edwards, a great-great-grandfather to whose church the Whitney family belonged, might well have approved. And it is important to note the effect of this attitude on Whitney's experience in Germany. He is only "tolerably happy" and definitely "not so high up in the air." Yet he retains the full force of his commitment. And he does it by making his commitment specifically a matter-of-fact affair of application rather than ideology.

The state of "wholesome humility" which kept Whitney's nose to the grindstone was entirely self-imposed. He was progressing well in his studies. Every day he would hear two or three lectures and have one or two private sessions with his instructors. During his first winter in Berlin he also worked hard at translating one of the published Vedas, learning Persian and Arabic, and working on his own article on English phonetics. The regularity of his habits is most formidable. His entry for New Year's Day of his second winter in Berlin reads: "Saw the old year out & the new in over a hymn of the Veda."[15]

There is also a mercenary quality to his devotion which is demonstrated in another diary entry of his first year:

The grand idea on my mind tonight is that I have got to pay Bopp five Friedrich d'ors, twenty-nine thalers nearly, for the time I have spent with him. I am utterly astounded, & if there were any stronger expression I would make use of it. 29 thalers for what has been worth no more than as many groschen to me! to think of the books that might have been purchased with so much money; & how ill my second quarter's account will look with such a spot on it! I have had the last experience with the old gentleman, & never really want to see his face again. . . . Bopp's lecture this afternoon, stupid enough as usual.[16]

This was a common and important episode for American students. Many, when they discovered that one or another of the famous professors they had traveled three thousand miles to hear was not worth even the low fee, felt completely duped and packed up. Bopp was notorious, and intellectually speaking, Whitney's complaint was certainly justified. But he took it with his usual good sense, writing to his friend Bumsted:

Two of the men on whom I had leaned rather hard proved rather broken reeds; one of them I have cut already, & the other I shall get rid of in two or three weeks. One of my instructors, Dr. Weber, a very young man, & the only one of whom I had never heard until I came here, turns out to be a "brick", & when after Christmas I take "privatissima" with him, I shall get along much better.[17]

As he predicted, he did get along much better. And the confidence and self-assurance of that prediction is entirely representative. It allowed him to be critical of himself as well as others, and gave him a sure sense of the personal moral standards that his work demanded: "Abel [a German tutorial mate] was not there again, & I went thro' everything alone. I am fast losing my confidence in him, & coming to regard him as a man of words rather than deeds."[18]   He then continues with a piece of self-criticism: "I fell upon the Ramayana & finished the first chapter, not reading it however, not reading it in a very thorough or scholar like way."[19]

The conjunction of the two criticisms is revealing. The criterion of "scholar like" by which Whitney judges himself is essentially the same as the Calvinist standard of devotion and duty and action in the world by which he judges his friend. The faintly hedonistic tone of the verb "fell upon" is interesting. It is as though Whitney had indulged himself carnally in a way that he should not have, and that he would be punished for it, or even that he would punish himself for it: he did in fact reread the passage. The self-confession of the last time is a typical example of how his Calvinist sensibility and values were applied to his secular scholarship in a way that Bancroft's Calvinism was not.

There is a certain ineffectuality and irony in the elder Josiah Whitney's advice to his son:

And now before I close, I must say a few words of vital importance, about which you know that fathers feel a deep solicitude in relation to their children. You will be exposed to various evil influences in a foreign land. Scientific men & literary men are peculiarly apt to overlook the one thing needful—I hope you will be on your guard—and admit no taint of German rationalism or German infidelity.[20]

This was virtually the same advice that Moses Stuart had dispensed to generations of American students. But for William Dwight Whitney it was almost beside the point. He had not lost his religious principles, merely displaced them into his scholarship with no hint that the transposition had been either difficult or troubling. He was not only able (supremely able) to research, decipher, edit, and analyze what most pious Christians even of his day considered pagan literature, but he gave every indication of enjoying it and of deriving a certain amount of religious inspiration from it. He did attend church frequently, however, and was especially appreciative when he came upon lusty congregational singing.

The problem of disbelief was still an issue for many parents of American students at mid-century, but it was no longer quite as feared as it had been a generation before. And neither was the trip to Germany itself so much of a strange venture into the unknown. Whitney, of course, had the benefit of his older brother's experience. But the number of men who had returned from German universities was now large enough that anyone seeking advice could easily find it. Only twenty years before Theodore Woolsey had had to get most of his advice on practical matters from unreliable travel books which he found after he arrived to be rife with mistakes and hearsay. And these were of no help academically. Although in 1850 there were still misconceptions about matters such as how long it took to understand an oral lecture in German (one minister from New Hampshire thought that a dozen years of intense study would hardly suffice),[21] most students could get accurate practical advice on these things before they left home.

Indeed, the growing familiarity of Americans with the German university experience was now beginning to breed problems of another sort. When Whitney arrived in 1850, there was a sizeable group, or "colony," of American students in both Berlin and Göttingen. The Americans not only knew of each other's existence, they roomed together and generally associated only with each other. Although many firm friendships were formed in this way, many of the Americans themselves recognized the danger of the exclusiveness of their social contact. Two decades before, Woolsey had intentionally removed himself to Bonn, where he knew there were no compatriots, mostly to escape an American friend (whom he sincerely liked). He complained that even with only one other American in the town, he was not meeting enough Germans or speaking the language. By Whitney's time, when anywhere from ten to twenty Americans could be in residence at any one time and a number of other American families more or less permanently installed, not to mention the increasing stream of American tourists, the problem was much worse. "That which I find standing most in my way here," Whitney complained,

is the number of American acquaintances I have in the city. We must of course be very social & friendly with one another (that is to say there are two coteries here, a northern and a southern, the members of which are on the most familiar terms with one another, & instantly polite to the other party) & we go sightseeing with one another, & take tea at one another's rooms so often that all the time that one can possibly spare for such things is quite used up, & none is left to cultivate German acquaintances. The consequence is that I have hardly heard a word of German since I came into the country.[22]

Whitney was not exaggerating. It required a conscious effort to make German acquaintances and almost a deliberate shunning of other Americans to speak much German. James Hart was one of the very few Americans to live with a German family and speak German constantly. But this only lasted one semester. Whitney did not make any close German friends until he went to Tübingen, where no American had been before. There, although he found most of the German students to be highly obnoxious, he cultivated a few friendships that he kept for life.

Whitney was an "inner-directed" person, and the conviction that sprang from within was sufficient to deal with the frustrations and anxieties of German study. He was not a victim of the psychological dilemmas which had plagued the first generation of American students. For him, the work itself was sufficient; American conviviality was a nuisance.

But for most of the other Americans this socializing was not only pleasant but necessary. It was part of a whole fabric of convention that was beginning to envelop the experience of studying at a German university. The Americans established strong social groups and conventions which, for most, served the same purpose as Whitney's strong inner motivation.

Fifteen years after Whitney, the problem of American students socializing exclusively with Americans was pronounced enough to be the subject of explicit warnings. "Allow me to pass along this little piece of advice," wrote Professor Thomas Chase of Haverford to his old student, Clement Smith:

—namely—to associate as much as possible with *German* students, eat at their tables, get into their sets, and fall into their ways. Of course it will be pleasant always to meet Americans, but beware of having thy time monopolized by them. One's object in travelling abroad, is to get away from America & surround oneself with new scenes & associates & influences.[23]

The old Quaker professor knew what he was talking about. But Smith, like most of the other Americans then, completely ignored the advice. The Americans at Göttingen (where he studied) had always been even more numerous and socially cohesive than those of Berlin, despite the movement between the two schools. As James Hart recalls, "We saw a great deal of each other, and we were in the main what might be called 'a jolly set.'"[24] Professor William Goodwin of Harvard had pointed out, in his letter of advice to Clement Smith, that there were "so many advantages apart from the University"[25] at Berlin. Despite, or more likely because of, the restrictions on cultural attractions at Göttingen, however, a highly developed social life evolved among the American students there. Every American from the time of Ticknor was recorded in the "Colony Book" which was the special responsibility of the "Patriarch" of the colony, the longest remaining member. For more than a half-century a large group of Americans continued eating at the Krone, whose venerable owner could recall the exploits of generations of American students.[26] Other tradesmen welcomed the American business: typically, Americans spent more than any but the richest German students. Herr Deuerlich, the bookseller, remembered two of his best customers, Francis Child and George Lane, for many years, and continued to send them books.[27]

By tradition the Americans stayed together as a group. Many took long walks together every day. They had for many years the reputation of being the best skaters in town, and a number of them practised ardently. One semester two complete baseball teams were fielded, and the Germans were treated to a strange sight. Few of the Americans participated in German fraternity drinking or duelling rites. But they compensated with their own rituals and celebrations, often a combination of German and American practises. For many years the Fourth was celebrated with heroic drinking contests. And throughout the year they would attend the weekly Kaffeeconcerte en masse. Often they felt the need for even more celebration, as James Hart recorded:

In addition to the Kaffeeconcerte, the work of the winter of 1863–4 was enlivened by a number of private social gatherings among the Americans. Our colony numbered, as I have said, ten. It was a curious phenomenon that no less than six of the ten had their birthdays to celebrate during the three months of December, January, and February. It would be ungracious of me to insinuate that the calendar had been tampered with. When a countryman surprised me at my books, staying long enough to help himself to a fresh cigar, and stated in an offhand way, that he would be glad to have the pleasure of my company the next Saturday night, at such a place, in honor of his birthday—'merely a few friends'— of course the only thing to do was to put on a smiling mien and make the best of it. But it *was* remarkable that a birthday should come around regularly every fortnight, to say nothing of the convenience of its always happening on a Saturday.[28]

Even at such cosmopolitan universities as Heidelberg, the Americans tended to stick together, and on any summer after- noon (the summer semester always attracted a large number of Americans from the other German universities to Heidelberg) a group of eighteen or twenty of them could be counted at one outdoor cafe.[29]

Later students at Göttingen or elsewhere knew nothing of the perplexities and difficulties which had faced their predeces- sors. Good practical advice about how to live, where to travel, and what seminars to attend was easily available, as Professor Goodwin advised Clement Smith: "As to living in a place like Göttingen, you usually find Americans who will put you on the right track."

"The right track" could also refer to a certain standard of behavior that the community could enforce. This social pressure did not often take an obvious form, but it could. The case of the Mason brothers illustrates what the community could do if some of its members took advantage of the distance from home to kick up their heels. The stern Berlin "Colony" not only refused to participate in their activities, primarily excessive drinking, they also made no secret of their disapproval. There was even a move within the community to write to the parents and have them bring the miscreants home. Eventually, however, the older Mason departed, and the younger brother, left by himself and socially ostracized, showed signs of reform. The other Americans, now mostly removed to Göttingen, seemed at first disinclined to accept this. "It is reported that the youn- ger Mason is coming here—do you know anything about it?" inquired Charles Joy of his former roommate, Whitney. "We

think it your duty to keep him in Berlin," he continued.[31]
Whitney, more critical but also more kind and forgiving than
the others, wrote back:

He has been wasting his time, absolutely here in Berlin, to be sure, but
it is to his credit that he has seen it, & is tired of it, himself, & is trying
to make his escape to a place where he can turn over a new leaf, & do
better.[32]

And he added with gentle sarcasm,

I hope you fellows down there who have such a faculty for putting men
forward on the course they ought to walk, will hold out a helping hand
to him. He won't do any harm to your company, however much you
may think yourselves a band of 'unequalled & unapproachables'.[33]

When Mason finally did come down to Göttingen, Joy wrote
back that the profligate had "commenced well," and continued,
"it was a good move his coming here & I think will be beneficial
to him."[34]

The social sanctions which the community displayed on this
occasion and several others are an important indication of its
strength and cohesiveness. The existence of such a powerful
group at two and then more of the German universities is a
definite sign of the social forces at work in this intellectual migration. For the colonies gave the Americans much needed
help—social, academic, and psychological—in coping with a
difficult and stressful situation. In emergencies they were vital.
When Clinton Camp suddenly took ill at Göttingen in 1852, one
of the group volunteered to nurse him and accompany him to
Italy. Others did everything they could, lending money and
contacting friends and relatives. Whitney journeyed down from
Berlin to Dresden to bring him his passport and some more
money.

There was, however, a limit to how much the colonies could
do for their members. An emergency like that of Clinton Camp
did not happen very often. And there was only so much information and help that communities could provide. Mostly, the
colonies existed for mutual psychological reinforcement. More
revealing than the Clinton Camp emergency was something that
happened during Clement Smith's first semester at Göttingen.
Smith told the whole story to his sister:

I think I mentioned in somebody's letter the arrival of an American named Tomilson here during the holidays. He turned out to be a curious case. After wandering around for a week or two like a restless spirit staying at the Krone at night, he at last took a room at Frau Heinze, with whom several Americans live; she had to give up her dining room to accommodate him, but he wanted to come so much, she said she at last consented to it. Well he stayed there just one week, seeming to be very miserable all the time. He was more homesick than anything else, I should think from what I have heard of the matter. If he had gone to work at once he probably would have gotten over it; but he did not. He seemed to have no mind of his own, and was continually asking the other Americans what they thought he had better do—curious in a man of over twenty-five. They advised him of course to go to work, but he did not do so, and at last became so miserable that his friends advised him to go home, which advice he did take, and set out for America on two hours notice, having occupied his room for just one week.[35]

What is remarkable in this story is not simply the lengths to which the colony went to help or the limits of their tolerance, but rather the unanimous advice they gave to the unfortunate Tomilson: "They advised him of course to go to work." In other words, there was an obvious and straightforward path to the higher learning that consisted mainly in submerging oneself immediately in the day-to-day business of whatever one wanted to learn. What a different attitude from that of the Americans at this same university only a half-century before! The earlier Americans had immersed themselves in their subjects, of course; there was no other way of learning a large amount of difficult material. But they did not have the same kind of easy assurance. Would these later Americans have told George Bancroft to go home after a week? He had asked the same forlorn question, "What should I do?" for two years.

The easy reliance on convention was no accident. Studying in Germany had become infinitely more familiar by the middle of the century. After the Napoleonic wars, the German universities with their strange students and customs had become regular tourist stops, and many travel writers included one or two as a regular feature. Often the accounts of the actual procedures and requirements of the universities were sketchy or inaccurate, while the tales of student exploits could be quite fabulous. By the 1840s, however, articles and whole books had appeared in both England and America exclusively on the sub-

ject of the German universities. Most of them still dwelt at
length on the ever-fascinating subjects of student costumes and
customs, and gave a great deal of attention to the *Burschen-
schaften*. Others were more intent on analysis of the German
academic system as a whole. Between these two extremes, an
abundance of solid information became available to prospective
American students.

The development of fast transatlantic steamship service combined with railway networks did even more to break down the
geographical as well as financial barriers to study in Germany.
In addition, increasingly easy facilities for transferring money
abroad (the first students had to rely on clumsy and inconve-
nient letters of credit on American merchants in London or
Paris) and rapid mail service facilitated travel and study. Until
the age of steamship and rail, an American student was cut off
from family and friends for months at a time. A letter could
take from six weeks to six months to negotiate the passage.
Later American students had no idea of the hardships and depression which this simple deprivation caused.

The result of all of these developments was to facilitate the
transition from America to Germany. Clement Smith noted in
his diary that it was not until he reached his hotel in Göttingen
itself, that he "truly felt like a stranger in a strange land."[36]
He had been brought to Göttingen so rapidly (by nineteenth-
century standards) that he had not yet experienced the inevitable cultural shock with which the Americans of a few decades
earlier would have contended for weeks or months before
reaching their German destinations. That Smith did not truly
feel as if he were in a foreign country until he reached Göttingen itself did not mean that he would escape cultural shock
entirely: German customs and styles were still very different
from those of America. But the shock was far less.

The cultures were not dissimilar as they had once been. And
the later Americans had less opportunity than the first to get
to know German ways. The German universities, and particularly Göttingen and Berlin, attracted large numbers of foreign
students, and the professors and townspeople were not concerned with them unless they came from a very unusual place.
The first Americans had complained of being treated as a "kind
of raree show." The Germans had literally expected to see

savages from the North American forests. But after a few decades they were left pretty much alone. The only German home that most of the Americans saw was a boardinghouse where the majority of the other inhabitants were Americans. Few had John Motley's opportunity to associate with a Bismarck in one of the exclusive fraternities or Hart's experience in a German family. Clement Smith wrote to his family that he couldn't tell them much about a German Christmas because most of the activity took place within the family, and neither he nor any other of the Americans was invited into one. They spent the day visiting each other.

If the later Americans remained outsiders to German culture, they still had to survive for several years in the middle of that society. The colonies, like the "nations" of the medieval universities, were a necessary response and a functional social institution. Often they not only protected the Americans from having to function by themselves in German society, they also reaffirmed their American values and made them more secure: "We Americans are growing so numerous here now that we shall soon be ready to vote the King quietly out of power & take the government into our own hands & teach 'em how people govern themselves,"[37] boasted Whitney after a year in Germany.

But the isolation and protection which the colonies fostered had a more serious effect on the studies of the American students. Rather than being as closely associated as formerly with German professors and students of their own subjects, they had a much closer social tie to other Americans, whatever the subject of their studies. Clement Smith exclaimed to his sister:

I am beginning to think there are more American students in the German universities studying Medicine or Chemistry and Engineering than any other branch. It is certainly so here. I am the only one studying Philology; there are two theology and one Law student; all the rest work in the dissecting room or in the laboratory.[38]

This was in Göttingen, the home of humanistic scholarship! The consequence for Smith was that he was noticeably less involved with his subject (while in Germany) than he had been or was to be. The same is true of Andrew Dickson White, a gifted and committed student and scholar. The only experience within a German classroom which he recounts is his famous anecdote of the aged Ranke mumbling to the ceiling,[39] and this despite the fact that White had also studied with Lepsius, Boeckh, Von Raumer, and Ritter, to mention only the most famous. The same lack of involvement is recorded by G. Stanley Hall, at least on his first visit of three years.[40] He enjoyed himself immensely and sampled a great deal of German learning, even working hard in a few stretches. But a commitment did not come until his second visit.

The Americans tended to be increasingly self-sufficient, even academically. It was seven months before Clement Smith paid his first social call on a German student.

Just before tea I called on Werth, and met in his room another Philolog to whom I have spoken often in Lecture but whose name I have not yet learned. Werth proposed I should give him some help with his English, which he wished to learn to speak, and in return he might do something for me. I declined of course.[41]

Now Smith, though perhaps a little shy, was not an unsocial person. He had many friends among the Americans and called on some of them every day. It is significant that he did not even know the name of the German student, despite having spoken to him in class a number of times. It is even more significant that he quickly refused social contact (despite his old professor's advice) of a kind that most of the Americans who had gone before him had welcomed. Why did he decline "of course"? He does not say. His German was not perfect and could have used practise. Perhaps he did not like this particular person; but there is no indication of that in his diary. Smith apparently seemed to need no more social contact; he did not feel that the opportunity to be closer to his German fellows was important, even though there was not a single other American student of philology with whom he could discuss his work. The social relations he had within the American colony were apparently sufficient, as they were for most other Americans.

Nor did Smith seem to feel a need to explore German culture in the same way earlier Americans had. Despite the fact that his German was not by any means perfect and that he had very little knowledge of the literature or history, he was perfectly ready to give up these studies within a few months of coming to Göttingen:

I had not intended to take any more lessons in German, but on calling on Professor Curtius the other evening, and informing him that I had given them up, he almost gave me a scolding, and impressed on me so forcibly the advantage of studying German literature now that I began to take lessons again forthwith. "Latin and Greek," he said, "you can study your life long, but now is the only opportunity to study the German literature, and to become acquainted with the manners and customs of the people." All of which seemed to me very sensible.[42]

It had not taken near-scoldings from eminent professors to make this piece of advice seem sensible to previous American students. And they did not have to depend on a knowledge of German literature "to become acquainted with the manners and customs of the people."

Smith's attitude was far from atypical. Hart records with disapprobation his countrymen's lack of effort in acquiring German:

Nine of ten Americans who study in Germany regard a knowledge of the language as only the means to some ulterior object, generally a knowledge of chemistry or medicine. It is not surprising, then, that they reduce their preliminary study to a minimum, in order that they may begin what they consider their real work as soon as possible. They are satisfied with learning enough grammar to recognize the connection of words in a sentence; the technical words of their science, which are to them the all important ones, they know by actual practice; all others are relatively unimportant. They read a play or two of Schiller, some of Goethe's poems, perhaps a few of Uhland's or Heine's. Of the language as an entirety, of German literature as a body of thought, they have but a very inadequate conception.[43]

Many of the Americans after mid-century were much less close to their professors than the earlier American students had been. It was unusual for someone like Curtius to take the time to admonish a young man whom he only saw among dozens of others in his lectures. For Smith attended only lectures (*privat,* the university not the public lectures) and not the more exclusive seminars or tutorials (*privatissima*) where the real teaching and learning went on. As a matter of fact, when he was approached to join the philological seminar, he was put in a rather embarrassing situation:

This morning I called on Leitsch to tell him I had decided not to enter the Seminar, but he strongly advised me to do so. Then I called on Sauppe and had quite a talk with him. He offered to criticize a dissertation if I chose to write one, and did not join the seminar. I am at a loss what to do.[44]

Smith was less at a loss what to do than what to say. He did not want to admit that he had no intention of ever writing a dissertation and planned only to stay at Göttingen for another six to eight months at the most. It was not a question of money. His father, an exceedingly wealthy Pennsylvania physician and gentleman farmer, was willing to let him stay as long as he wished. And it was not a question of being bored with his studies or unable to do them. He had learned a great deal from Curtius and Sauppe and had taken magnificent lecture notes to which he referred throughout his long teaching career at Harvard. It was not his commitment to scholarship that was in question. He simply lacked that sense of being in the one place in the world where authentic and ineffable Truth could be revealed.

As late as the 1840s young Transcendentalists like Charles Stearns Wheeler[45] still came to Germany with that sense. Even to Smith the history of Greek and Roman art was exciting and certainly new. But he was looking forward more eagerly to seeing the real thing in Italy and Greece. Curtius's lectures were incisive and helpful, but at no time did Smith give any indication that he expected any sort of divine revelation from them. Though he was grateful to learn about Hesiod's *Theogony* from Wiesler and took copious notes, neither he nor many of the other Americans who studied philology in Germany in these decades after mid-century seemed to believe that these studies were the sole source of humanistic authenticity. He certainly did not think of any of the books he read in the same way as the earlier Americans had thought of Wolf's *Prolegomena.* Though he appreciated the importance of the Justinian code and Roman constitutional history, and though they made Roman history more meaningful for him, he did not have any sense that this understanding was vital to the preservation of the American Republic or the efflorescence of its arts and letters. It was simply another course which he attended, listened to intently, and made full notes on. This is not to imply that Smith did not work hard. He got up early in the morning, spent most of the day in classes or reading, and put in most of his evenings copying and reviewing notes and preparing.[46] Commitment was not lacking; but it was more restrained and of a different sort.

German scholarship, too, had changed significantly from the time when the first Americans had come to Göttingen. In fifty years lectures and seminars had become infinitely more specialized and separated from each other. Philology had once been a unitary discipline, bringing together isolated antiquarian interests and scholarly pursuits like numismatics, archaeology, and art history, and focusing them. The historical perspective it engendered was common to the higher biblical criticism, as well as the study of law. And the vision that justified this historical perspective was a unitary vision which aimed at capturing that ineffable Herderian spirit of each of the ancient cultures, making the ruins and fragments speak with the life of the past. This was the vision which drew and often sustained the first American students even when they could not assimilate this kind of scholarship and bring it back to the New World.

By the time Americans were ready to absorb the German form of scholarship *wie es eigenlich gewesen,* that scholarship had changed. It had become less visionary and far more specialized. And this very change made it much easier for the Americans to assimilate. They had evolved social and psychological defenses to help them survive in Germany. These allowed them to work hard and absorb large amounts of specialized knowledge and techniques. The later Americans were not bothered by the discrepancy between ideal and reality that had so upset people like Bancroft.

Nor did they have to fear, like Everett and Bancroft, that their specialized learning would not have a market back home. By mid-century the prestige of German training was secure. As little as a year of it commanded respect and often instant offers of employment. Harvard had pointed the way by sending its professorial appointees for their training to Germany. Yale, when it made Woolsey's training the immediate excuse for his appointment, seemed to concur. By 1850 many universities made it publicly known that they would favor applicants with German training. "There should be two chairs provided for in the Romanic and in the Gothic languages to be filled by Americans who have prepared themselves for their work in Europe,"[47] proclaimed the European-trained president of Yale—Woolsey—in that year. It is important to note that Yale announced this criterion of hiring long before it had turned into an identifiably modern university. Harvard was, if anything, even more partial to German-prepared scholars in the humanities. Before Yale had raised the funds for even one of the two projected chairs, Harvard had hired Francis Child and George Lane. By the 1860s the most influential portion of its faculty had German training.

The increasing numbers of Americans returning from the German universities to academic positions in the United States could only help ensure even more positions for those who came afterward. And this came to be one of the most important functions of the American colonies at the German universities. They started to function something like old-boy networks. Clement Smith was sent to Göttingen by his "old-boy" professors, who promptly hired him on his return. Whitney was encouraged by Edward Salisbury and James Hadley, who lobbied long and effectively for Yale to snap him up as a professor of Sanskrit.

If an American university would not pay expenses in Germany and the student himself could not afford to go, that was not an insuperable barrier. As G. Stanley Hall tells the story, Henry Ward Beecher had only heard second-hand of the young man's desire to study abroad. While working in a small town as a substitute pastor, he received a letter asking him to come immediately to Beecher's home in Brooklyn. After some questions

he gave me a sealed note to the lumber magnate, Henry Sage, the benefactor of Cornell, which I presented at his office without knowing its contents. To my amazement, after some scowling and a remark to the effect that his pastor took amazing liberties with his purse, he gave me a check for one thousand dollars. Taking my note to repay it with interest, he told me to sail for Europe the next day and never trouble him again. I wrote my resignation to Coudersport [where he had been substitute

pastor], sailed for Europe the next day, and never saw Mr. Sage afterwards but paid him the principal and interest from my earliest savings
some years later.[48]

When Hall returned from this first period of German study,
he was promised a position in a large midwestern university.
On the president's learning of Hall's actual studies, however,
the offer was rescinded on the grounds that such subjects
would hopelessly corrupt the students.

Francis Child had no such trouble with Harvard. And his
actions following his appointment as the first professor of
English at Harvard mark the beginnings of an "old-boy" net-
work among the returning American students themselves.
Immediately he began lobbying not only for his friend George
Lane, who joined him as Latin professor the following year,
he also worked hard to bring Whitney along:

I shall always hope to have you for a colleague & that at no distant date:
for you are one of the few of any country (those that I have known)
who understand what scholar and scholarship mean. The East must be
represented at Cambridge & I shall at once commence preparing the
way.—You, Lane & I—if we could all work together in Cambridge &
accomplish something for the university, the land & learning . . . I shall
be really happy.[49]

Child returned to accomplish a great many things for "the
university, the land & learning." But he did not make himself
into the kind of German scholar he had mocked so devastat-
ingly in his letters to his friends. He had distanced himself too
well from the "spreading tree" of philology.

He was as good as his word to Whitney, however. But Harvard moved too slowly. Yale, despite the absence of any funds
for a position, was determined to get Whitney. It was an important precedent. For in committing itself to Whitney, Yale
also committed itself to modern academic scholarship.

Whitney was perhaps the first American scholar in the
humanities whose work was unquestionably on the level of his
European contemporaries and who was accepted by them as
an intellectual equal. The strength of his own intellect and will
is singularly impressive; for others with talents nearly as great
as his had preceded him without having found a way to use
their gifts in the service of scholarship or even to make use of

their German training, or, in many cases, even to assimilate or appreciate it. The obstacles they faced were both external and internal. By Whitney's time some of the external impediments had been removed—it was certain physically and financially far easier to study abroad than it had been. What Whitney did was to overcome some of the internal barriers to the assimilation of German scholarship.

And what Whitney did for himself through his own strength, the social context of the American colonies helped subsequent American students to do. They helped them to weather the problem of culture-shock, supplied the need for social contact, alleviated homesickness and depression, provided security and commonsense guidance, and served as an invaluable employment contact. They also helped to insulate Americans, not only from German culture, but also from the kind of visionary idealism which misled the first generation of Americans in Germany. They helped to focus energy in conventional and specialized ways. That German scholarship had evolved in this direction only abetted this trend among the Americans.

The conventionality which became a growing part of the American experience at the German universities made this study into a normative period of preparation, particularly after German study became recognized and generally rewarded. In the absence of graduate schools at home, the German universities came to serve precisely that purpose, at least in the years after the Civil War. Whitney's Horatio Alger optimism turned out to be amply justified. And when America was ready for the new scholarship, there was a large cadre of trained men who could define the needs of the scholarship and fulfill its demands.

Conclusion

At its best Germany gave young Americans a commitment to scholarship as a profession.

—Jurgen Herbst,
The German Historical School in American Scholarship

"In any known civilization there will be found something in the way of esoteric knowledge,"[1] begins Thorstein Veblen's brilliant and perverse book, *The Higher Learning in America*. And the following paragraphs reinforce this apparent disparagement of the historical as well as ontological singularity of modern scholarship:

The Higher learning as currently cultivated by the scholars and scientists of the Western civilization differs not generically from the esoteric knowledge purveyed by specialists in other civilizations, elsewhere and in other times. It engages the same general range of aptitudes and capacities, meets the same range of human wants, and grows out of the same impulsive propensities of human nature.[2]

Veblen concedes soon enough, however, that the modern university and what he holds to be its essential purpose—the pursuit of knowledge—are both historically recent and unique. Moreover, he admits, its scope, method, canons, and tenets are profoundly different from those of other cultures and peculiarly adapted to particular modern habits and "canons of reality." Yet he marvels at the fervor the "objective" character of modern scholarship still inspires:

this highly sterilized, germ-proof system of knowledge, kept in a cool, dry place, commands the affection of modern civilized man no less unconditionally, with no more afterthought of an extraneous sanction, than once did the highly personalized and highly mythological and philosophical constructions that had the vogue in the days of the schoolmen.[3]

Veblen suggests that although the "canons of reality" to which this (like any other "esoteric" knowledge) must subject itself for verification, are historically conditioned, this historicity does not subvert but grounds scholarship as a value system. He not only does not care that the values which he so vehemently espouses for the Higher Learning in America are historically limited, he glories in it, and in his contention that both scholarship and the institutions that support it are founded on nothing more than "habits of thought." As he states:

An institution is, after all, a prevalent habit of thought, and as such it is subject to the conditions and limitations that surround any change in the habitual frame of mind in the community.[4]

Veblen thus changes what is merely social and historical into something that is essentially grounded in the social and historical. His insistence on the priority of habit and custom in the historical development of institutions is close to that of Weber. Though Veblen appropriates the words *vocation* and *vocational* as the polemical objects of this treatise, it is clear that he regards scholarship itself as a vocation unto itself, intimately connected both with modern society and the modern university. Though his brief prefatory remarks on the historicity and social origin of scholarship do not in themselves constitute a sociology of learning, they do raise important historical problems of such a study. And among these one of the most puzzling is the development of the peculiar and particularly modern form of scholarship and the sense of vocation which feeds it.

The modern form of academic scholarship in the humanities is a specific creation of the nineteenth century. That it is a structure dependent on both specialization and hierarchy in its social and intellectual constituents is at the same time obvious and surprising: obvious as an analogy with the emergence of specialized and hierarchical bureaucratic forms in both business and government, and surprising contrasted to the prevailing democratic and holistic intellectual movements of the nineteenth century and to the unitary claims of the humanities themselves. The mechanistic spirit and the value placed on research have often been blamed on the influence of the sciences, whose investigative precepts are said to have been forced on the humanities. The truth is otherwise. The essential para-digs of modern academic scholarship in the humanities developed long before the modern form of academic research in the sciences. These forms and ideals were laid down by the German classical philologists at the end of the eighteenth century. The German philologists not only achieved stunning methodological breakthroughs that advanced their own work, they also created a new sense of their work as constituting an academic discipline, or field. From the beginning this sense of field and of the necessary work of research depended on an immense degree of specialization. From the beginning it created a barrier between the scholar and the "outsider."

Academic study in the humanities began with a vision of a new humanistic authenticity and a concept of advanced philological scholarship as the key to this essentially historical understanding. It depended not only on the visionary effusions of Winckelmann, but even more on the revolutionary understanding of the classical world-view and classical mythology developed by C. G. Heyne and his pupils. It was this "truer" and more "authentic" understanding of the social and intellectual workings of ancient societies that Herder and Humboldt were able to use in a more popular way. They were able to fashion bold and brilliant speculations from Heyne's hard-won breakthrough.

But in the hands of Heyne's most brilliant pupil, F. A. Wolf, this understanding was put to a far different use. Unlike Herder and Humboldt, he did not apply these insights to his contemporary world or use them to foster cross-cultural comparisons. Rather, he applied his understanding of the workings of Homeric society, as well as his immense specific knowledge of classical literature and history, to the subject of classical studies itself. Like scientific experimenters more than a century before, Wolf destroyed the old paradigm of scholarship in the humanities and substituted a new form. That form depended both on a new style of question making as the principal activity of an academic scholar and of a conception of a defined but constantly expanding "field" of classical literature and history.

If Wolf was not the first to employ the label *Altertumswissenschaft,* he was surely the first to give it a viable meaning, by making it into the first identifiably modern academic discipline in the humanities. He did this by making research and discovery, not initiation into a closed body of knowledge, the primary goal of an academic philologist. He did not make education itself secondary, but changed its meaning and organized it around the process of research that he had pioneered; in other words, he made higher education into an initiation in "creating" knowledge by mastering the techniques by which the "frontiers" of knowledge were first defined, and then explored and enlarged.

That Wolf had as his best-known disciple such a brilliant academic propagandist and entrepreneur as Wilhelm von Humboldt only gave additional potency to his creation. For Humboldt assured that Wolf's paradigms were quickly translated into an institutional form at Berlin. Though the institutional structures of the German academic systems were by no means complete when the first Americans arrived on the scene, the intellectual force of German philological scholarship was clear and compelling. In terms of the values of the German system, the old American college seemed weak, inefficacious, and unauthentic.

Throughout the nineteenth century America sent thousands of students to study in the German universities. Virtually every one of the Americans who built the modern university system in the United States, and many of those who staffed the new institutions, studied in Germany. And most of these pioneers studied there before 1870. It was was in that period that the American commitment to scholarship as a profession was forged. It was then that Americans from every section of the country (except the Far West) came to Germany to study. And they brought back with them a vocation of scholarship.

This was not a gradual process, however, The American experience in the German universities was not uniform throughout this period. In fact, two distinct generations of Americans can be seen in the period 1815 to 1870. These two generations went through substantially different learning experiences in Germany. They tended to follow different vocational patterns, at least in the humanities. And they brought back different lessons from their German study.

The conventional view of the experience of the first generation of American students in the German universities is that they not only appreciated but assimilated the modern form of scholarship in the humanities, primarily in classical philology, which they found there, and that it was not until they returned home that they found their new studies could not take root in the rocky intellectual soil of Puritan New England. The last is true to some extent. But an examination of the experience of the first Americans in the German universities explicitly contradicts the view of most historians that they "had a splendid time of it" there. The Americans, far from assimilating German scholarship, experienced grave doubts and anxieties about it. And the first generation of Americans to study in the German universities seems not to have absorbed very much of German learning. What little they did assimilate was almost entirely confined to a conventional knowledge of modern and ancient languages. They seem not to have learned any of the startling new philological techniques which in many cases they had gone to Germany expressly to assimilate.

The reason for this surprising failure was not intellectual but psychological. The anxieties which the first generation of Americans experienced in the German universities completely prevented their learning what they had ostensibly set out to learn. And these psychological constraints were not noticeably provoked or exacerbated by religious differences or doubts. Nor did they spring primarily from the discrepancy between the ideals of German scholarship and its institutional and social reality. The Americans were under no obligation to replicate the German academic structures on the other side of the Atlantic, even were that possible, which they all knew it was not.

The psychological stresses and anxieties of the first group of American students in the German universities are difficult to interpret with confidence. But one thing is certain: they could not come to German scholarship and the German academic system as openly as they proclaimed and often believed. They came with the anxieties and self-doubts of the society that sent them. And they came under the influence of a powerful double-bind for which the solution was preordained. No matter how much they understood or admired the German scholars or the authentic knowledge which German scholarship gained, the Americans could not accept or assimilate this kind of scholarship or academic system. They drew back from it, circumscribing their studies not simply to what was safe theologically but to what was safe culturally and psychologically.

The American anxieties were not removed by the bridging of the gap between the ideal of scholarship and its reality in Germany. If anything, that gap widened as the century progressed and the social and intellectual forms of German scholarship became increasingly rigid and conventional, betrayed the unitary ideals of its founders, and grew increasingly specialized. Yet this did not appear to create additional barriers to American assimilation of German values. If anything, these trends may have made it increasingly easier for Americans to understand and absorb the new German values.

The Americans, for example, readily adopted the German maxim of the intrinsic connection between teaching and research. This had been first enunciated at a time when methodological breakthroughs had revolutionized knowledge and the process of creating knowledge in the humanities. Scholars who had pioneered in these advances were privy to a kind of learning radically different from that claimed by their predecessors. The connection between initiation into this process and participation in it seemed obvious. But what happened when these methodological advances slowed down or ceased? Was the connection between teaching and research so obvious when the increase in knowledge became merely quantitative and no longer qualitative? The Americans who finally absorbed German values never paused to ask themselves those questions.

The interminable debate over the retention of an elementary classical curriculum in the colleges had deferred the introduction of an advanced classical scholarship to the United States. The assimilation of the metaphors and values of academic research were likewise deferred until the second generation of Americans to study in the German universities. Yet their assimilation of the modern form of academic study did not proceed from any intellectual affinity with the sources of German scholarship. The experience of the second generation, if less traumatic, was more conventional in every way than that of the first generation. Approaching their German studies with a doggedly practical spirit, the Americans remained essentially closed to the original humanistic purposes of German philology.[5]

It is not quite fair to contrast German rhetoric with American practice. However, what few remnants of the rhetoric of

Neuhumanismus floated by Americans in their German seminars they tended to ignore or attribute to an unfortunate but entirely forgettable propensity for musty metaphysics on the part of their German teachers. It is significant that of hundreds of American students of the humanities who studied for periods up to four or five years in German universities, scarcely one (up to 1870) should have come back with a thorough grounding in German philosophy. Whatever thorough education Americans acquired in Germany tended to be exclusively on the practical side, with a few (increasingly) perfunctory obeisances to Goethe and Schiller.

Among this second generation of American students in the German universities, there were a surprisingly large number who achieved a certain scholarly equality with their European counterparts. William Dwight Whitney must, of course, be included in that number. His friend Francis Child, the great Harvard ballads scholar should also be named. Basil Gildersleeve, William Graham Sumner, G. S. Hall, and Horace Howard Furness (accounted the greatest Shakespearean scholar of his day) might also make the list. Germany had indeed given them (and dozens of others) a commitment to scholarship as a profession, as Herbst asserts. But that commitment did not, as he suggests, imply conversion to a new religion. The passionate espousal of a new creed of scholarship belonged to the first generation of Americans in Germany: to the callow Bancroft, the impressionable Henry Dwight, the immature Peter Porter and George Cabot Ward in their Heidelberg attic. The second generation came with a different spirit. Their "religion of research" was a faith of sober and conventional application to the details of their trade. Research was less a religion than a business practice to them. Like Twain's Connecticut Yankee, they brought their mercantile New England habits to the banks of the Necker and the Spree.

Throughout the first half of the nineteenth century in America, there were periodic calls for a committed republican scholarship to serve the interests of the new nation. Bancroft's vision of the new scholarship was forthrightly nationalistic. Emerson rejoiced that "our day of dependence, our long apprenticeship to the learning of other lands, draws to a close."[6] A follower and one of the only Americans of his day with a thoroughly German gymnasium education, Frederick Hedge heartily agreed and hailed the appearance of an American scholar who would be the moral reformer and literary muse[7] of the American republic. This was—not surprisingly—close to the cultural nationalism of *Neuhumanismus,* a cultural nationalism which provided not only the intellectual but the institutional roots of the modern German academic system.

Yet the connection between literary or cultural nationalism and the actual development of scholarship and institutions in America is considerably more difficult to make. American scholarship in the humanities was more distanced from a humanistic or artistic matrix such as had attended the beginnings of German scholarship. And it developed largely independently of any institutional context: the American college proved inhospitable, and the modern university did not develop until after American scholarship was well advanced. The assimilation of the modern form of scholarship was therefore much more the aggregate of individual American experiences abroad, the nineteenth-century settlement of the frontier of German knowledge. The issue of nationalism was less important to this kind of process than it had been to the state-initiated and state-supported German systems. Where intellectual and institutional developments comprise the history of German scholarship, the burden of American development is comprehended more by individuals, within the framework of individual experiences and psychology.

Very quickly, however, social and institutional patterns grew out of these German experiences. The second generation of American students were successful in constructing social and psychological mechanisms that allowed them to absorb some of the German learning. They were even more successful in constructing professional career patterns which allowed them to use their German training. The more prominent among them successfully built a new structure of learning, and dozens (and eventually thousands) of the others staffed these new institutions. The speed with which inner experience was transmuted into institutional form could not help but have an effect on the style of American scholarship. American institutions were not mere copies of European blueprints. But like the earliest Japanese imitations of Western technology and ideas, they tended to be mechanistic and rigid. By the middle of the nine-teenth century, scholarship as a profession implied specialization and research. These proved to be fatally easy for Americans to absorb. Scholarship as a profession was not the best that German tradition had to offer, but it was the best that Americans could assimilate. Between vision and vocation there can be no doubt which America chose.

Appendix

Statistical Tables of
American Students in German Universities

University Registrations by Decade

	Göttingen	Berlin	Heidelberg	Halle	Other	Total
1810–40	25	16	1	7	6	55
1840s	7	27	5	11	10	60
1850s	44	22	12	4	19	101
1860s	45	31	22	3	26	127
Total	121	96	40	25	61	343

Students in the Faculties by Decade

	Law	Medicine	Theology	Philosophy[a]	2x[b]	Faculty Unknown	Total[c]
1810–40	3	6	12	24(20;4)	4	–	41
1840s	2	3	14	26(18;8)	1	3	47
1850s	12	5	8	54(31;23)	1	3	81
1860s	10	17	8	54(20;34)	–	6	95
Total	27	31	42	158(89;69)	6	12	264

[a]The figures for the humanities and sciences respectively are given in parentheses.
[b]The same student in two columns. This refers to the numbers of students enrolling in more than one faculty, and is subtracted from the totals.
[c]This total refers to the actual number of students, since multiple registration is already accounted for in the 2x column.

Registrations in the Faculties by Universities

	Law	Medicine	Theology	Philosophy[a]	Double Regis-tered	Unknown	Total
Göttingen	17	9	15	79(38;41)	3	4	121
Berlin	8	8	18	63(45;18)	4	3	96
Heidelberg	6	2	2	26(12;14)	1	5	40
Halle	–	–	23	4(4;–)	2	–	25
Other	2	8	3	49(25;24)	1	2	61
Total	33	37	61	219(122;97)	11	14	343

[a] Figures for the humanities and sciences respectively in parentheses.

Multiple Registrations: Universities by Universities

	Göttingen	Berlin	Heidelberg	Halle	Other
Göttingen	81	23	8	5	17
Berlin	23	41	14	11	22
Heidelberg	8	14	17	–	10
Halle	5	11	–	11	2
Other	17	22	10	2	26

Multiple Registrations by Decades

	G/B	G/H	G/Ha	G/O	B/H	B/Ha	B/O	H/O	Ha/O
1810–40	5	1	3	3	–	5	3	–	–
1840s	4	–	1	2	1	4	2	2	1
1850s	7	3	–	4	3	1	5	4	–
1860s	7	4	1	8	10	1	12	4	1

G = Göttingen; B = Berlin; H = Heidelberg; Ha = Halle; O = Other.

Multiple Registrations: Faculty by Decade

	Law	Medicine	Theology	Philosophy[a]	Double Registered	Unknown
1810–40	1	1	7	9(7;2)	2	–
1840s	–	1	7	7(4;3)	–	–
1850s	1	1	1	19(12;7)	1	–
1860s	3	7	1	22(6;16)	–	1

[a]Figures for the humanities and sciences respectively in parentheses.

Registration in the Faculties by Universities for the Period before 1840

	Law	Medicine	Theology	Philosophy[a]	Double Registered	Total
Göttingen	3	3	7	15(14;1)	3	25
Berlin	1	1	7	9(7;2)	2	16
Heidelberg	–	–	–	1(1;–)	–	1
Halle	–	–	7	2(2;–)	2	7
Other	–	1	1	4(4;–)	–	6
Mobile Students	1	1	7	9(7;2)	2	16

[a]Figures for the humanities and sciences respectively in parentheses.

Registration in the Faculties by Universities for the 1840s

	Law	Medicine	Theology	Philosophy[a]	Double Registered	Unknown	Total
Göttingen	–	–	2	4(3;1)	–	1	7
Berlin	2	1	6	19(14;5)	1	–	27
Heidelberg	–	–	1	2(2;–)	–	1	5
Halle	–	–	11	–	–	–	11
Other	–	–	2	7(4;3)	–	1	10
Mobile Students	–	1	7	7(4;3)	–	–	15

[a]Figures for the humanities and sciences respectively in parentheses.

Registration in the Faculties by Universities for the 1850s

	Law	Medicine	Theology	Philosophy[a]	Double Regis- tered	Unknown	Total
Göttingen	8	2	2	31(15;16)	–	1	44
Berlin	1	1	3	17(14;3)	1	1	22
Heidelberg	2	–	–	10(7;3)	1	1	12
Halle	–	–	3	1(1;–)	–	–	4
Other	2	1	1	17(9;8)	2	–	19
Mobile Students	1	1	1	19(12;7)	1	–	21

[a]Figures for the humanities and sciences respectively in parentheses.

Registration in the Faculties by Universities for the 1860s

	Law	Medicine	Theology	Philosophy[a]	Double Regis- tered	Unknown	Total
Göttingen	6	4	4	29(7;22)	–	2	45
Berlin	4	5	2	18(10;8)	–	2	31
Heidelberg	4	1	1	13(3;11)	–	3	22
Halle	–	–	2	1(1;–)	–	–	3
Other	–	6	–	20(8;12)	–	–	26
Mobile Students	3	7	1	22(6;16)	–	1	34

[a]Figures for the humanities and sciences respectively in parentheses.

Region of Colleges by Decade

	Harvard[a]	Yale[a]	New England	New York	Middle Atlantic	South	Midwest	Total
1810–40	15	4	9	2	6	3	–	39
1840s	11	5	11	5	5	3	–	39
1850s	25	14	15	4	2	4	1	65
1860s	22	29	11	14	2	4	2	84
Total	73	52	46	25	15	14	3	228

[a]Harvard and Yale are listed separately because they sent such a large proportion of the sample.
[b]There were 36 unknown.

Registration in the Faculties by College Regions

	Law	Medicine	Theology	Philosophy[a]	Double Registered	Unknown	Total
Harvard	9	11	10	44(32;12)	6	5	73
Yale	6	7	6	31(13;18)	–	2	52
New England	2	1	17	25(14;11)	1	2	46
New York	2	4	1	17(9;8)	1	2	25
Middle Atlantic	–	2	3	9(4;5)	–	1	15
South	5	3	1	4(2;2)	–	–	13
Midwest	–	–	–	2(2;–)	–	1	3

[a]Figures for the humanities and sciences, respectively, in parentheses.

College Regions by Time after Leaving College or Professional School

Years	Harvard	Yale	New England	New York	Middle Atlantic	South	Midwest
Under 2	52	31	23	17	4	5	–
2–10	15	16	16	5	7	8	3
Other	3	2	5	3	4	1	–
Total	70	49	44	25	15	14	3

Time after Leaving College or Professional School by Decade

	Under 2	2–10	0	Total
1810–40	20	13	4	37
1840s	22	13	3	38
1850s	39	20	7	56
1860s	55	28	5	88

Region of Origin by Decade

	New England	Middle Atlantic[a]	South	Midwest	Total
1810–40	23	10	5	–	38
1840s	23	12	7	1	43
1850s	45	20	8	3	76
1860s	45	34	6	3	88
Total (19 unknown)	136	76	26	7	245

[a]This column now includes New York State.

Regions of Settlement by Regions of Origin

	Settlement								
Regions of Origin	*New England*	*Middle Atlantic*	*South*	*Mid-west*	*West*	*Europe*	*Un-known*	*Total*	*oo*[a]
New England	87	44	4	21	8	15	16	185	136
Middle Atlantic	15	51	4	7	4	7	15	103	76
South	3	8	13	3	1	3	8	39	26
Midwest	2	1	–	5	1	–	1	10	7

[a]"Out of" - the number of students involved; does not total a column.

Regions of Settlement by Regions of Settlement: Students from New England (of 137 students)

	New England	*Middle Atlantic*	*South*	*Midwest*	*West*	*Europe*
New England	54	25	1	10	5	9
Middle Atlantic	25	12	–	12	3	8
South	1	–	2	1	–	–
Midwest	10	12	1	6	4	1
West	5	3	–	4	2	1
Europe	9	8	–	1	1	3

Regions of Settlement by Regions of Settlement:
Students from the Middle Atlantic States (of 76 students)

	New England	Middle Atlantic	South	Midwest	West	Europe
New England	7	7	1	1	–	3
Middle Atlantic	7	33	3	5	3	4
South	1	3	–	–	–	–
Midwest	1	5	–	4	1	2
West	–	3	–	1	1	–
Europe	3	4	–	2	–	1

Subsequent Occupations by Decade

	a	l	c	md	b	f	O	u	Total	oo
1810–40	21	3	7	5	1	–	12	4	53	41
1840s	24	4	12	5	2	–	12	5	64	47
1850s	51	9	5	5	6	1	15	6	88	81
1860s	59	9	5	11	8	1	18	6	117	95
Total	155	25	29	26	17	2	57	21	322	264

a = Academic career; l = Law career; c = Clergyman; md = Doctor; b = Business career; f = Farmer; O = Other; u = unknown; oo = out of

Notes

Abbreviations of Manuscript Sources

DCT Dartmouth College, Ticknor Collection
HAS Harvard Archives, Smith Collection
MHSB Massachusetts Historical Society, Bancroft Collection
MHSE Massachusetts Historical Society, Everett Collection
NYPLC New York Public Library, Cogswell Collection
YLW Yale Library, Whitney Collection
YW Yale Library, Woolsey Collection

Introduction

1. *The German Historical School in American Scholarship* (Ithaca, 1969), p. 2.

2. Ibid., p. x.

3. "The Prussian Universities and the Research Imperative" (Ph.D. diss., Princeton University, 1973). I regret that the relevant portions of the present work were written before Mr. Turner's work was available.

4. Lawrence Veysey, *The Emergence of the American University* (Chicago, 1965), p. 127.

Chapter 1

1. *Life, Letters and Journals of George Ticknor* (Boston, 1876), p. 24.

2. MS letter to H. W. Longfellow, July 24, 1836, Longfellow MSS, Houghton Library, Harvard University.

3. *Life, Letters and Journals of George Ticknor,* p. 101.

4. Ibid.

5. Georg Iggers in Leopold von Ranke, *The Theory and Practice of History,* ed. Georg Iggers and Konrad Moltke (Indianapolis, Ind., 1973), p. xxxv.

6. Lawrence Veysey, in *The Emergence of the American University* (Chicago, 1965), uses the concept of research as the major characteristic of the modern university. It is, however, too slippery for him to nail

down and leads to much tedious repetition in his argument. See also Steven Turner, "The Prussian Universities and the Research Imperative" (Ph.D. diss., Princeton University, 1973).

7. Friedrich Paulsen, *Geschichte des gelehrten Unterrichts auf den deutschen Schulen und Universitäten,* 2d ed. (Leipzig, 1897), vol. 2.

8. See Robert Clark, *Herder: His Life and Thought* (Berkeley, 1955), pp. 67 ff. and 188 ff., and Rudolf Haym, *Herder nach seinem Leben und seinen Werken* (Berlin, 1880), pp. 528–32. See also Georg Iggers, *The German Conception of History* (Middletown, Conn., 1968), and Karl Mannheim, *Essays in the Sociology of Knowledge* (London, 1952), pp. 124–33, for a discussion of historicism and modern scholarship.

9. Cf. Ranke's remark that "each epoch is immediate to God."

10. Clark, p. 67.

11. See Joseph Ben-David and Awraham Zloczower, "Universities and Academic Systems in Modern Societies," *European Journal of Sociology* 3 (1962):64–84, for the best discussion of the emergence of the competitive, decentralized university system. See Leonard Krieger, *The German Idea of Freedom, History of a Political Tradition* (Boston, 1957), for a discussion of the political uses of historical research in Herder's time. Steven Turner has the best account of the development of the research ideal.

12. Herder was certainly not the only German of the era to decry "todte Gelehrsamkeit." Goethe and Lessing launched frequent sallies. Even the most scholastic of German professors, F. A. Wolf, professes an antischolasticism that is far from perfunctory.

13. *Gesammelte Schriften* (Berlin, 1903), vol. 2.

14. Heyne called for the "Bildung des Geschmacks und Veredlung des Gefühls"; quoted in Paulsen, 2:35 and 39.

15. See E. M. Butler, *The Tyranny of Greece over Germany* (London, 1935), for a somewhat hysterical discussion of Goethe's "Dämon" in his *Poetry and Truth.*

16. *Sämmtliche Werke,* ed. Hellen (Stuttgart, 1904), 1:261.

17. J. M. Gesner, quoted in Paulsen, p. 19.

18. *Kleine Schriften* (Halle, 1869), vol. 2. R. H. Robbins, *A Short History of Linguistics* (London, 1967), pp. 151–53, holds this conception of language to be fundamental to modern linguistic study and follows Edward Sapir's "Herder's 'Ursprung der Sprache,'" *Modern Philology* 5 (1907–08):109–42, in tracing it from Herder to Humboldt. This idea may have been mediated by Heyne and his student F. A. Wolf, Humboldt's teacher. See also Holger Pedersen, *The Discovery of Language,* trans. J. W. Spargo (Bloomington, Ill., 1962).

19. *The Enlightenment* (New York, 1968), 1:69.

20. See Butler and Walter Rehm, *Griechentum und Goethezeit* (Bern and Munich, 1968), and, much better than either of these, Henry Hatfield, *Aesthetic Paganism in German Literature* (Cambridge, Mass., 1964).

21. See Humboldt, 3:188 and 10:90, for examples of the young and the old Humboldt, respectively. Santayana's dark irony captures but does not explain this infatuation: "How dignified everything was in those heroic days! How noble, serene and abstracted! How pure the blind eyes of the statues, how chaste the white folds of the marple drapery. Greece was a remote, fascinating vision, the most romantic thing in the history of mankind," *Three Philosophical Poets* (Cambridge, Mass., 1910), p. 175.

22. Gay, 1:39.

23. See Eduard Spranger, *Wilhelm von Humboldt und die Humanitäts-idee* (Berlin, 1909), pp. 5ff. for a discussion of the centrality of the concept of *Bildung* in Humboldt's work.

24. *The Logic of the Humanities* (New Haven, 1961), p. 21.

25. Hatfield, p. 3.

26. *Paideia: The Ideals of Greek Culture* (New York, 1945), 1:xxiii.

27. See Spranger for the ideal of creativity in Humboldt.

28. See, for example, Humboldt, 3:188.

29. Quoted in Paulsen, 2:169–70.

30. Arnold Heeren, *Christian Gottlob Heyne* (Göttingen, 1813), p. 114.

31. See Krieger, pp. 86–125, for a specific discussion of Kant's influence within a contemporary intellectual context.

32. See Friedrich Paulsen, *Die deutschen Universitäten und das Universitätsstudium* (Berlin, 1902), and W. Lexis, *Das Unterrictswesen in deutschen Reich* (Berlin, 1904), vols. 1 and 2, for histories of the German university in this period.

33. See Lexis and Paulsen, *Die deutschen Universitäten.*

34. See Cassirer, *Logic*, p. 19, and Hajo Holborn, *History and the Humanities* (New Haven, 1972), for a discussion of this link.

35. Holborn, pp. 23–26.

36. Ibid., p. 25.

37. *Encyklopädie und Methodologie der philologischen Wissenschaften* (Leipzig, 1877); quotations in English are taken from the abridged translation by J. P. Pritchard, *On Interpretation and Criticism* (Norman, Okla., 1968), p. 12.

38. Ibid., p. 13.

39. *Grundriss der Philologie* (Landshut, 1808), p. 1.

40. Ibid., p. 10.

41. Ibid., p. 9.

42. Ibid., p. 3.

43. Boeckh, p. 12.

44. Ast, p. 12.

45. See Mannheim for a detailed discussion of the relationship between German Idealism and the modern form of scholarship in the humanities.

46. Professor Ernst Bratuschek, in the introduction to the German edition of Boeckh, p. iii.

47. He does say, however, that "Philology is the source of knowledge, surely no small thing," p. 13.

48. G. P. Gooch, *History and Historians in the Nineteenth Century* (Boston, 1959), p. 30, remarks very justly that Boeckh succeeded brilliantly in "an objective reconstruction of a vanished world," in the *Public Economy of Athens*. Lord Acton, in his "German Historical Schools," *Historical Essays and Studies* (London, 1907), p. 350, called that same work "about the only history produced before the critical epoch [1824-28] which still stands, unshaken and erect."

49. Quoted in Holborn, p. 26.

50. This recalls Boeckh's claim for philology (see n. 47 above). But even a twentieth-century historian, G. P. Gooch, p. 26, calls Wolf's *Prolegomena ad Homerum* "one of the cardinal books of the modern world."

Chapter 2

1. Steven Turner, in "The Prussian Universities and the Research Imperative" (Ph.D. diss., Princeton University, 1973), has written a definitive external history of the development of modern scholarship. This chapter will be concerned mainly with internal changes.

2. (Halle, 1795); hereafter referred to as the *Prolegomena*. Wolf made explicit his definition of classical studies and his conception of "field" in other, more technical studies. I have chosen to focus on a work that is more popular and contains his ideas in a more implicit form.

3. Translated by Hermann Muchau (Leipzig, 1908). All citations are to this German edition. All quotations are given in German except in one or two instances in which I have also cited the Latin because the exact working of the original was striking or important.

4. See *F. A. Wolf: Ein Leben in Briefen,* ed. S. Reiz (Stuttgart, 1935), pp. 185-86.

5. *Prolegomena,* p. 154.

6. For the reaction to the *Prolegomena,* see Richard Volkmann, *Geschichte und Kritik der Wolfschen Prolegomena zu Homer* (Leipzig, 1874), pp. 70ff., and Conrad Bursian, *Geschichte der classischen Philologie in Deutschland* (Leipzig and Munich, 1883), pp. 526ff.

7. On Homer's place in the *Querelle,* see Donald M. Foerster, *Homer in English Criticism* (New Haven, 1947), pp. 5-25.

8. Humphrey Trevalyan, in *The Popular Background to Goethe's Hellenism* (New York, 1934), claims the existence of massive antihellenism in the first three-quarters of the eighteenth century. His claims seem a little overstated and his findings apply only to the study of Greek language and literature in the original. Friedrich Paulsen's statistics on the editions of Homer in the original, *Geschichte des gelehrten Unterrichts auf den deutschen Schulen und Universitäten,* 1st ed. (Leipzig, 1885), p. 320, neglect the many translations in the period which he and Trevalyan proclaim as "the lean years" of hellensitic interest. These numerous vernacular editions support the conception of Homer as a "modern vernacular" poet of the eighteenth century.

9. See M. L. Clarke, *Greek Studies in England, 1700–1830* (Cambridge, 1945), p. 124.

10. Even La Motte, Mme. Dacier's chief opponent in the *Querelle,* used and praised her translation.

11. See Norman Cullan's discussion of the seventeenth-century conception of Homer "as the Prince of Poets" in the Twickenham edition of Alexander Pope's *Poems,* ed. Maynard Mack (New Haven, 1967), 7:1xxi.

12. See Hugh Honour, *Neoclassicism* (Baltimore, 1973), for a succinct and accessible discussion of Homer's place in the neoclassical revival in art and for a small discussion of garden imagery in eighteenth-century Homeric criticism.

13. The utopian image of the Homeric world is reinforced in Mme. Dacier's criticism by her note that the age of Homer was the more beautiful insofar as it bore no resemblance to her own.

14. See Pope's preface to his translation of the *Iliad* in *Poems,* ed. Mack, p. 3.

15. J. E. Sandys, *A History of Classical Scholarship* (London, 1921), vol. 3, and Conrad Bursian. See also Arnaldo Momigliano, *Studies in Historiography* London, 1966); R. H. Robins, *A Short History of Linguistics* (London, 1967), Rudolf Pfeiffer, *A History of Classical Scholarship* (Oxford, 1976), vol. 2; Hans Aarsleff, *The Study of Language in England,1780–1860* (Princeton, 1967).

16. See Sandys, vols. 2 and 3, for a fairly comprehensive account of these kinds of activities.

17. Ernesti was particularly criticized for his arbitrary readings and methods. See Robert T. Clark, Jr., *Herder: His Life and Thought* (Berkeley, 1955), pp. 70–73.

18. The problem of Greece and the creativity of Greek culture is present throughout Herder's work from the beginning, in his "Über die neuere deutschen Litteratur; Fragmente."

19. (Edinburgh, 1735); hereafter cited as the *Enquiry.*

20. (London, 1767); all citations are to the London edition (3d) of 1824; hereafter referred to as the *Essay*.

21. Foerster claims the *Enquiry* as the first systematic study of Homer. Norman Cullan, on the other hand, claims that honor for the *Essay*. Both books were influential throughout Europe. Heyne used both in his seminar at Göttingen when Wolf attended; see Clemens Menze, *Wilhelm von Humboldt und Christian Gottlob Heyne* (Ratingen, 1966), p. 13. See also Wilhelm Körte, *Leben und Studium F. A. Wolf's* (Essen, 1833), p. 265, and Karl Borinski, *Die Antike in Poetik und Kunsttheorie* (Leipzig, 1924). Curiously, Sandys omits all reference to the *Enquiry* and except for an obscure footnote, to its author.

22. This was the society, remarked Walpole, "for which the nominal qualification is having been to Italy and the real one, being drunk." Wood was admitted on more substantial grounds.

23. *Poetry and Truth*, ed. M. S. Smith (London, 1913), 2:83.

24. See D. C. Allen, *Mysteriously Meant* (Baltimore, 1970), pp. 309–10, for a short discussion of Blackwell's advanced concept of mythology.

25. *Enquiry*, pp. 130 ff.

26. *Spicilogia antiquitatum Aegypti atque ei vicinarum gentium* (Glasgow, 1720).

27. *Enquiry*, pp. 109–10.

28. *Essay*, pp. 151 ff.

29. *Enquiry*, pp. 333–34.

30. *Essay*, p. 179. This conception of Homer as a shrewd copyist from nature may be found in Mme. Dacier, Pope, and Cowper, among others, in the eighteenth century.

31. *Prolegomena*, p. 94.

32. Ibid., p. 84. The chilly rules are often described as French, which supports Paulsen's conception of *Neuhumanismus* as partly an anti-French movement, *Geschichte des gelehrten Unterrichts* 2:7.

33. Heyne averred that there were probably fewer than a half-dozen positions for philologists in Germany at the time when Wolf proclaimed his intention of becoming one. See Menze, p. 13, and Körte, p. 265. Heyne makes his vocational view of the study of the classics clear in his "Verbesserungsvorschlage zur Hebung des Pädagogii zu Illfeld," in *Mitteilungen des Gesellschaft für deutsche Erziehungs- und Schulgeschichte* 4 (1894): 66. See also Friedrich Böhme, *Die formale Bildung des Intellekts in der Unterrichts Lehre des aufstiegenden Neuhumanismus* (Ph.D. diss. Leipzig University, 1912), for Heyne's views.

34. *Prolegomena*, p. 74. See also note 4 above. The notion of community is reinforced in small ways throughout the *Prolegomena*.

35. See J. A. Davison, "The Homeric Question," in *A Companion*

to Homer, ed. A. J. C. Wace and F. H. Stubbings (New York, 1962). Paulsen's assertion in *Geschichte des gelehrten Unterrichts,* 2:8, that the reevaluation of Homer "gegleitet und bezeichnet eine grosse Revolution in die aesthetischen Anschauungsweise der europäisher Völker," is something with which I agree, although not in the precise sense that Paulsen intended. I have already asserted that there was a surprising amount of continuity in the content of Wolf and his predecessors. It is something else in Wolf which inaugurates "eine grosse Revolution."

36. *Prolegomena,* p. 59.

37. See J. A. Davison, "The Homeric Text," in Wace and Stubbings, and T. W. Allen, *The Origin and Transmission of Homer* (Oxford, 1924), for detailed accounts of the Homeric manuscripts. See Pfeiffer, vol. 1, for an account of their ancient states.

38. *Prolegomena,* p. 153. See also pp. 129 and 158.

39. Ibid., pp. 60, 62, 139, 200, 201, and 203.

40. Ibid., p. 138.

41. Ibid., p. 129.

42. See Sandys, Bursian, and Volkman for definitions and histories of the Homeric question in the nineteenth century.

43. *Prolegomena,* p. 188.

44. (Berlin, 1807–10). This book, along with the seminar technique which Wolf helped establish, profoundly shaped classical studies as a modern academic discipline. The scholarly assumptions that permit this are certainly present in this book, as they may be in others of the period. The *Prolegomena* was, however, the primary and most important exposition of Wolf's views.

45. *Prolegomena,* p. 137.

46. Ibid.

47. Ibid., p. 64.

48. "Homer und classische Philologie," in *Werke* (Munich, 1956), vol. 3.

49. Heyne and Voss, among many others, felt this part of Wolf's character, as Wolf's letters to his friends in vol. 1 of *Ein Leben in Briefen* bear out. His letters to Heyne border on obsequiousness—until Wolf suddenly lets loose in his last vicious polemic.

50. See Tagebücher, quoted in *Goethe und die Antike,* ed. Ernst Grummach (Berlin, 1948), 2:150ff.

51. Ibid., p. 148.

52. See his letter to C. von Knebel and his diary entries for the years 1811, 1813, 1820, and 1821, in ibid., pp. 171ff.

53. Ibid., p. 146.

54. Ibid., pp. 148–49.

55. Humboldt named Wolf as "first among living philologists" in 1808, while Heyne was still alive; *Gesammelte Schriften* (Berlin, 1903), 10:17.

56. Wolf was appointed to the faculty as a "lesende mitglieder" rather than a professor.

57. Paulsen's judgment in *Geschichte des gelehrten Unterrichts*, 2:209, that "Wolf pflegt der Begrunder der Philologie als einer besonderen und selbstständigen Wissenschaft gennant zu werden," must stand.

Chapter 3

1. Francis Wayland, in his *Thoughts on the Present System of Collegiate Study in the United States* (Boston, 1842), for example, was careful to promote a certain diffidence of tone in his discussions of foreign systems of education. This did not save Wayland from some xenophobic criticism.

2. See Lawrence Veysey, *The Emergence of the American University* (Chicago, 1965), p. 126. The other major work on German influence, Jurgen Herbst, *The German Historical School in American Scholarship* (Ithaca, N.Y., 1969), also concentrates on these later students. Orie Long, *Literary Pioneers, The American Exploration of European Culture* (Cambridge, 1935), is the standard published account of the first four American students to study in Germany. Cynthia Stokes Brown, "The American Discovery of the German University: Four Students in Göttingen, 1815–1822" (Ph.D. diss., Johns Hopkins University, 1966), is a more recent, thorough study based on manuscript sources. See also Henry Pochmann, *German Culture in America* (Madison, Wis., 1957), pp. 66–77, and Thomas Wentworth Higginson, "Göttingen and Harvard Eighty Years Ago," *Harvard Graduates Magazine* 6 (1897):6–18. I picked the year 1870 as my stopping point for three reasons: (1) most of the pioneers of the American university had been educated by then; (2) by that year several American graduate schools had begun to compete with the German universities; and (3) the numbers of American students rose enormously after that year.

3. Herbst, pp. 7–8.

4. In another place Herbst asserts that "The primary appeal of the German universities was quite clearly in their specialized scholarship," ibid., pp. 18–19. This may not be accurate with regard to the earlier group of Americans.

5. Ibid., p. 6.

6. Daniel B. Shumway, "Göttingen's American Students," *German Historical Review*, vol. 3 (June 1907).

7. Heidelberg, like Berlin, appears to have attracted students for

pursuits other than study, although the number of these who actually matriculated at the university was probably rather small.

8. United States Bureau of Education, "Notes on the History of Foreign Influence upon Education in the United States," *Reports of the Commissioner*, 1 (1897–98):591–632.

9. James Morgan Hart, *German Universities: A Narrative of Personal Experience* (New York, 1974), was the first reliable account of study at a German university. It was not, however, the first actual account of German universities. English popular guidebooks from the beginning of the nineteenth century carried descriptions of the universities and fabulous accounts of student fraternities and duels. Henry Dwight's *Travels in the North of Germany* (New York, 1829), the first American narrative, offered a great deal of substantial information to the prospective student, along with some criticism of American education that was rather bitterly resented at home. By the 1840s the literature describing German universities was already extensive. William Howitt's *The Student Life of Germany* (Philadelphia, 1842), is typical. It advertised itself as containing forty of "the most famous student songs." More serious accounts were also available by the 1850s. Philip Schaff, *Germany: Its Universities, Theology, and Religion* (Philadelphia, 1857), was one of these.

10. Much more work remains to be done with the published registration records of all the German universities, among them the records of Heidelberg, *Die Matrikel der Universität Heidelberg* (Heidelberg, 1884–1916).

11. *German Universities*, pp. 158–59.

12. *Die Matrikel der Universität Heidelberg*, vol. 6.

13. The average number of universities attended for all German students may be under two. Americans appear to have been almost as mobile as German students.

14. "German Influence on American Historical Studies, 1884–1914" (Ph.D. diss., Yale University, 1953), and Charles F. Thwing, *The German and the American University: One Hundred Years of History* (New York, 1928), pp. 40–42.

15. Neither James Morgan Hart nor G. Stanley Hall, *Life and Confessions of a Psychologist* (New York, 1923), mention any large number of Americans in the 1860s.

16. See Shumway.

17. See Hart and the MS letters of William Dwight Whitney, Whitney Collection, Yale University Library.

18. See J. Conrad, *Das Universitätsstudium in Deutschland* (Jena, 1884), p. 25, for figures on the relative decline of enrollments at Halle and the other German universities. See also Friedrich Paulsen, *Die deutsche Universitäten und das Universitätsstudium* (Berlin, 1902).

19. Evidently, the ethnic motivation of the Pennsylvania Dutch did not

bring many of them to German universities in this period, for there are very few such names in the sample.

20. Hall recounts the story of Henry Ward Beecher ordering Henry Sage, a wealthy philanthropist, to lend Hall one thousand dollars in *Life and Confessions,* pp. 182–83.

21. Henry Torrey, H. W. Longfellow, George Bancroft, Edward Everett, James Russell Lowell, and George Ticknor are some of the people Harvard paid to study in Germany.

22. Edward Everett's Ph.D. was honorary, confirmed because of his position as a professor in a postsecondary institution of education.

23. The founders and first editors of *The Atlantic Monthly* and *Scribner's* had studied in Germany. For extensive accounts of this kind of German "influence," see Pochmann.

Chapter 4

1. Within a few weeks of residence in Germany, Edward Everett was hard at work deciphering the Wolfian controversy; see Edward Everett to Alexander Everett, 15 September 1815, Edward Everett Collection, Massachusetts Historical Society. (Henceforth this collection will be cited as MHSE.) Bancroft had not even landed in Europe before Everett wrote to him of Wolf; see Edward Everett to George Bancroft, 18 May 1818, MHSE. There are numerous entries in George Bancroft's diary referring to Wolf, the lengthiest being that of 3 October 1818, MS Diary of George Bancroft (hereafter cited as Bancroft Diary), in the Bancroft Collection, Massachusetts Historical Society (hereafter cited as MHSB).

2. MS Diary of George Ticknor (hereafter cited as the Ticknor Diary), 12 September 1816, Ticknor Collection, Dartmouth College (hereafter cited as DCT).

3. George Bancroft to Andrews Norton, 14 December 1818, MHSB.

4. Edward Everett to George Bancroft, 15 March 1819, MHSB.

5. *Synopsis of a course of lectures on the history of Greek Literature* (Boston, 1824?).

6. Everett, for example, is able to deal with the dilletante questions and arguments of Thomas Jefferson with ease; see Edward Everett to Thomas Jefferson, 29 February 1824, MHSE.

7. Edward Everett to Alexander Everett, 1 December 1816, MHSE.

8. Bancroft to Kirkland, 1 February 1821, MHSB.

9. See Jerry Brown, *The Rise of Biblical Criticism* (Middletown, Conn., 1969), for an account of the reception German theology met with in the United States.

10. *Three Centuries of Harvard, 1636-1936* (Cambridge, Mass., 1965), p. 226.

11. *George Ticknor and the Boston Brahmins* (Cambridge, Mass., 1967), p. 85.

12. *George Bancroft: Brahmin Rebel* (New York, 1944), p. 29.

13. "Göttingen and Harvard Eighty Years Ago," *Harvard Graduates Magazine* 6 (1897):17.

14. "The American Discovery of the German University: Four Students in Göttingen, 1815–1822" (PH.D. diss., Johns Hopkins University, 1966), p. 305.

15. Tyack, p. 58.

16. See Jerry Brown for Stuart's career and his assimilation of German theology. See also Sydney Ahlstrom, *A Religious History of the American People* (New Haven, 1972).

17. Moses Stuart to Edward Everett, 12 August 1812, MHSE. Jerry Brown has an amusing account of the auction of Joseph Buckminster's library, from whence came some of the German books. Everett and Stuart evidently bid against each other.

18. Moses Stuart to Edward Everett, 24 June 1814, MHSE.

19. Ibid., 25 September 1813.

20. Ibid., 12 September 1814.

21. Ibid.

22. Edward Everett to Theodore Lyman, 1 March 1816, MHSE.

23. Ibid.

24. Edward Everett to Alexander Everett, 5 January 1816, MHSE.

25. Ibid., 1 December 1816.

26. Eichhorn (among others) corresponded with Everett for years and terrified subsequent American students with tales of his brilliance.

27. He wrote to his brother, "Except my French and German lessons, I have none now but Greek." 16 June 1816, MHSE. In the same letter he makes much of being allowed to stay for two more years and, in fact, says "I have determined to stay at all costs." Yet, even though permission came readily enough, Everett did not stay.

28. George Bancroft to Edward Everett, 4 August 1818, MHSB.

29. Ibid., 12 September 1818.

30. George Bancroft to Andrews Norton, 5 September 1818, MHSB.

31. Ibid.

32. Harvard Corporation Minutes, Harvard University Archives, September 1817.

33. Edward Everett to George Bancroft, 14 October 1818, MHSB.

34. Edward Everett to Alexander Everett, 5 January 1816, MHSE.

35. George Bancroft to Edward Everett, 14 November 1818, MHSB.

36. Bancroft's language may have been dictated by simple courtesy or the desire to please; these are psychological strategies, too.

37. George Bancroft to John Kirkland, 17 January 1819, MHSB.

38. Bancroft writes: "You charged me on leaving you to become a

good biblical critic and a philologian; but to be good in either of these branches, I must devote myself particularly to either one of them, and carry on the other as a mere secondary affair. Which of these shall I choose?" Ibid.

39. Ibid.

40. John Kirkland to George Bancroft, 26 May 1819, MHSB.

41. George Bancroft to Edward Everett, 1 August 1819, MHSE.

42. In his letter to Everett (ibid.), Bancroft makes it seem as if he were defying Kirkland to study with Gesenius at Halle, when in fact it had been Kirkland's suggestion. Bancroft asserts that he had "got more theology or quite as much of it as can be used in America," but fervently maintains that "this abandoning theology is not to be thought of." He then enquires about the possibility of studying history.

43. Ibid.

44. Edward Everett to George Bancroft, 23 August 1819, MHSB.

45. Ibid.

46. George Bancroft to Andrews Norton, 10 July 1819, MHSB.

47. It is a game which may have the classic characteristics of the approach-avoidance conflict.

48. There is a youthful exuberance in Bancroft's language; this does not, however, explain his protracted psychological maneuvers.

49. See George Bancroft to his father, 3 October 1818, MHSB.

50. Bancroft Diary, 30 September 1818, MHSB.

51. George Bancroft to Andrews Norton, 5 September 1818, MHSB.

52. Bancroft objected strenuously to Eichhorn's penchant for the scatological. Everett and Ticknor, equally priggish in many respects, did not react nearly so strongly. George Calvert, a few years later, positively liked Eichhorn, *First Years in Europe* (Boston, 1866), p. 116.

53. See George Bancroft to Edward Everett, 1 August 1819, MHSB.

54. George Bancroft to Andrews Norton (?), 9 March 1820, MHSB.

55. See p. 79 above.

56. George Bancroft to John Kirkland, 26 October 1818, MHSB.

57. George Bancroft to Andrews Norton, 9 January 1819, MHSB.

58. George Bancroft to John Kirkland, 15 January 1820, MHSB.

59. Kirkland had quoted with approval, "With us, commerce, manufacturing, all that is profitable, all that is mechanical, and all that is sensual, will take care of itself; and it is the rock on which the glory of America may split, that everything is calling her with siren songs to a physical, inelegant, immature, unsanctified, Carthaginian, perishable prosperity." "Literary Institutions—Universities," *North American Review* 7 (1818):274.

60. Everett, whose advice on educational reform Kirkland had solicited earlier, knew precisely how to play on the president's anxieties on the

subject. In a twenty-seven-page epistle—one of his earliest and most successful "orations"—he had used the image of commercial decadence with deadly effectiveness: "But still the gentlemen say, we do not want the books. What do we then want? do we want literature? do we want Science? do we want knowledge to be in the land; do we want something to be written that will give a tone to the nation, that will create some general taste in the people, that will furnish our children something to boast of? Or do we love this illiterate [*pace* the Phoenician alphabet] Phoenician prosperity—this glory of ships entered, & ships cleared, this dispensation of newspapers and pamphlets—this invariable report of Logbook, and . . . of frigate & Seventy-four; of bales and packages; of tobacco & Rice, aye of Cod haddock & lumber? Are we pleased that New England is famous in Europe, chiefly for her pickled beef?" Everett to Kirkland, 19 April 1817, MHSE.

61. As though Everett's repeated image of America as the modern Phoenicia were not strong enough, he could be even worse: "Oh that my dear stupid land would awaken from her unblessed Carthaginian commercial torpor . . . !" he exclaimed on one occasion. Edward Everett to Robert Walsh, 29 December 1817, MHSE.

62. Commercialism is an odd charge for a New Englander to hurl at a German.

63. George Bancroft to John Kirkland, 2 April 1820, MHSB.

64. Some of the responsibility for this tainting of German scholarship should rest with Bancroft's brother, who kept up a steady barrage of moralizing throughout Bancroft's entire stay in Germany; see John Bancroft to George Bancroft, 7 July 1819, Bancroft Collection Cornell University Library.

65. Both Pochmann (pp. 73-74) and Brown (pp. 43-44) suggest that these reactions were purely personal.

66. (Boston, 1876).

67. The Ticknor diary is completely unlike the Bancroft diary, both in tone and penmanship.

68. Ticknor Diary, vol. 1, 10 September 1816.

69. Ticknor's notes in his diary indicate that he was not in the least dissatisfied with his own performance. He worked hard and mastered a great deal; see Ticknor Diary, vol. 1, 6 April 1816.

70. Ticknor Diary, vol. 3, 22 March 1817. The anxiety posed by the erudition of the Germans is considerable in Ticknor's case. He writes frequently also of the "mortifying distance" between a European and an American "scholar."

71. J. G. Cogswell to Stephen Higginson, 13 July 1817, Cogswell Collection, New York Public Library (hereafter cited as NYPLC).

72. George Bancroft wrote to Kirkland, "He studied, & became sick,

& studied & became about dead & yet studied" (10 October 1818, MHSB). Everett had written to Ticknor the year before, "You ought to write to Cogswell not to kill himself through want of exercise, sleep, & food, as he is visibly doing" (8 June 1817, DCT). Cogswell was seriously ill in Germany.

73. J. G. Cogswell to Stephen Higginson, 13 July 1817, NYPLC. Cogswell is not reticent about mentioning his own depression in his letters to Bancroft, Everett, and Higginson.

74. Moses Stuart to T. D. Woolsey, 4 April 1827, Woolsey Collection, Yale University Library (hereafter cited as YW).

75. See T. D. Woolsey to Sarah Woolsey, 21 April 1828, YW, for an extensive moral analysis of the French and German nations.

76. T. D. Woolsey to William Woolsey, 28 March 1830, YW.

77. Woolsey's antipathy to his cousin is not the sole cause for his opposition to Dwight's ideas on education and the German university system. Woolsey's angry reaction to Dwight's *Travels in the North of Germany* (New York, 1829), is considerably greater than the difference in their ideas would warrant.

78. Woolsey unburdened his soul in a number of long letters to his college friend, Arthur Twining. In one of these he speaks of the comfort which philological scholarshiop provides him, in contrast to "the weary waste of feelings" over his lack of Christian virtue; yet most of the time he appeared hostile to philological scholarship. See T. D. Woolsey to Arthur Twining, 7 July 1828, YW.

79. Bancroft speaks often of the loneliness and the pain of separation from his family; see George Bancroft to Andrews Norton, 9 April 1820, MHSB: "The sort of life I lead here will teach me to bear solitude well." A few months later he writes, "I may get in fact a long fit of nostalgy—a sad disease, that has it's [*sic*] seeds in the most vital organs around the heart, and manifests itself in an ugly feeling of vacuity." Ibid., 6 July 1820.

80. George Bancroft to Andrews Norton (?), 7 January 1819, MHSB.

81. Edward Everett to Robert Walsh, 29 December 1817, MHSE.

82. Less than ten years after the first Americans studied in Germany, Woolsey was to exclaim on the decay of Latin in the classrooms in Germany; see T. D. Woolsey to William Woolsey, 1 January 1828, YW.

83. Morison, p. 226.

84. Nye, p. 21.

85. Ibid., p. 72.

86. Van Wyck Brooks, *The Flowering of New England, 1815–1865* (New York, 1937), p. 37.

87. Morison, p. 228. Nye states (p. 63), "President Kirkland, while a progressive and a liberal, wished to move slowly, sifting the good from the harmful, adapting to Harvard's uses only that which it needed and

might readily assimilate." This appears to be somewhat of a transposition of modern attitudes and labels into the past.

88. Cogswell was under no illusions as to just who had frustrated his efforts to improve the Harvard Library and turn it into a real university library. He stated quite openly and bluntly to Kirkland: "I have been doubting for a long while if it were not wrong for me to be here; my views of education differ too much from yours, from those of the gentlemen of the corporation, to allow my efforts for the advancement of the institution ever to be meaningful." Harvard Corporation Papers, Harvard Archives, 21 October 1822. In the same letter he said, "I cannot persuade myself that the opportunities I have enjoyed are turned to good account by devoting myself to labour, which might as well be performed by any shop boy from a circulating library." The responsibility for defining Cogswell's duties lay with Kirkland. It was he who failed completely to take advantage of Cogswell's unique background and education, and indeed would not allow him to use it.

89. See Herbert Peukert, *Die Slawen der Donaumonarchie und die Universität Jena 1700–1848* (Berlin, 1958).

90. George Bancroft to Andrews Norton, 16 September 1820, MHSB.

91. Ibid.

92. *Main Currents in American Thought,* vol. 2: *The Romantic Revolution in America, 1800–1860* (New York, 1954), p. 429.

93. *American Intellectual History and Historians* (Princeton, 1966), p. 15.

94. As Bancroft confesses to Norton (9 February 1820, MHSB), "My studies of late have limited themselves almost entirely to learning tongues." Everett made the same admission to Theodore Lyman (1 March 1816, MHSE): "What I have been acquiring here is principally Greek." Ticknor and Woolsey learned little else beside languages.

Chapter 5

1. "The Utility of Classical Learning," *North American Review,* vol. 19 (July 1824). According to Russell Nye, *Society and Culture in America, 1830–1860* (New York, 1974), p. 4, "Since it had rejected England, the nation turned to Greece and Rome (particularly to Rome, the most powerful republic in history) for symbols it might adapt to its own uses." America appropriated the ancient symbols but could not assimilate the modern classical philology.

2. Nye, p. 4.

3. Ibid.

4. Ibid.

5. Emerson waxed poetical on the effects of Everett's lectures in

Boston: "Germany had created criticism in vain for us, until 1820 . . . when Edward Everett returned from his five years in Europe, and brought to Cambridge his rich results."

6. Robert Bridges Patton, *A Lecture on Classical and National Education* (Princeton, 1826), p. 4.

7. Ibid., p. 20.

8. Ibid., p. 19.

9. Ibid., p. 16.

10. See Richard Hofstadter and Wilson Smith, *American Higher Education: A Documentary History* (Chicago, 1961), pp. 276–91, for an easily accessible abridgment of the 1828 Yale Report. The report affirms that "if we have not greatly misapprehended the design of the patrons of and guardians of this college, its object is to *lay the foundation* of a *superior education* . . ." (p. 278, italics in the original). In other words, the primary obligation of American higher education was to its least rather than its most advanced studies.

11. Josiah Quincy, Sr., *Remarks on the Nature and Probable Effects of Introducing the Voluntary System in the Studies of Latin and Greek* (Cambridge, Mass., 1841), p. 9. The reaction to the president's ideas was not favorable; see *North American Review* 54 (January 1842):35 ff.

12. Ibid., pp. 13–14.

13. Ibid., p. 8.

14. Ibid., p. 10.

15. Ibid., p. 12.

16. Ibid.

17. *North American Review* 52 (April 1841):510.

18. In fairness it should be mentioned that the demand for advanced classical study was stimulated in Prussia by the state-imposed, philologically based curriculum in the gymnasia and by the preparation of teachers for secondary schools.

19. Bristed's fatuous tone may be judged by the opening sentences of the review: "The Bostonians are justifiably proud of themselves, and justly so, on many accounts. Their high standard of morality is undoubted; equally undoubted are their social virtues; their enterprise is most commendable, and few would be disposed to deny them a large amount of general information and much learning, of the 'Society-for-the Diffusion-of-Useful-Knowledge' sort. Unfortunately, the best men often fall into strange delusions." *The Knicker-Bocker* 29 (June 1847):543. Bristed had unique credentials as a reviewer, having studied at Cambridge for five years beyond his American B.A. But his review was full of the most picayune, niggling criticisms. After quoting Felton's remark, "The opening scene represents the palace of AGAMEMNON, at *Argos,*" Bristed exclaims: *"Mycenae,* Mr. Professor, *Mycenae! Mycenae!!"* The *North American*

Review was so incensed by Bristed's rude (and mostly inconsequential criticisms, that it broke a long tradition and replied directly to the review, vol. 67 (July 1847), pp. 239-55, citing numerous errors on Bristed's part. The real question about the merits of Felton's edition was why American scholarship on the highest levels still had not progressed beyond school editions. The answer to this may have been too obvious to squabble over.

20. 28 October 1814, MHSE.

21. John Cassin to Joseph Wright, 8 September 1865, Harvard Archives, Smith Collection.

22. Eliot wrote to his mother from Göttingen, "thankfully I shall get into a pleasant region once more & have nothing further to do with Göttingen Professors." Samuel Eliot to Catherine Eliot, 5 July 1822, Harvard Archives, Eliot Collection.

23. George Haven Putnam (the publisher) remarked that "making the European round . . . was considered desirable for the American college graduate before he should settle down to the work of business or of a profession." *Memories of My Youth, 1844-1865* (New York, 1914), p. 116. But this applies more to the American students who did not take the trouble to matriculate in a German university.

24. Unfortunately, his published correspondence does not supplement his fictionalized accounts of German university life.

25. Wheeler sent back an unusual series of six letters to Emerson, three of which were published nearly verbatim in *The Dial,* vol. 3, nos. 3, 4, pp. 388-97 and 541-44. All of the letters contain large amounts of detailed information and gossip concerning university life and study in Heidelberg and Berlin in the early 1840s.

26. *Harvard Memorial Biographies,* vol. 1 (1866), p. 96.

27. See Leon Howard, *Victorian Knight-Errant, A Study of the Early Career of James Russell Lowell* (Berkeley, 1952), for a detailed account of Lowell's early struggles in the literary market.

28. According to Russell Nye, Edgar Allen Poe did more than handsomely from his magazine work, receiving from four to five dollars a page from Graham's (*Society and Culture in America,* p. 77). By 1858, Everett had been offered $10,000 from Sylvannus T. Cobb for a single work (ibid., p. 69).

29. For the fight for Eliot, see Samuel Eliot Morison, *Three Centuries of Harvard, 1636-1936* (Cambridge, Mass., 1965), pp. 323-29.

30. Francis Child to Francis Parkman, 18 April 1869, Massachusetts Historical Society, Francis Child Collection. Child's support may have been critical in overcoming the fears of the classicists toward Eliot's appointment. See Morison, p. 327. Eliot's elevation was preceded by a report of a committee of the overseers which showed substantial agreement with Eliot's published views, *The Atlantic Monthly* 23 (1869):

Notes to Pages 116–128

203–20, 358–67. The chairman of the overseer's committee was James Freeman Clarke, who had himself studied theology in Germany.

31. See Jerry Brown, *The Rise of Biblical Criticism* (Middletown, Conn., 1969) for an account of the acceptance of German higher criticism in America.

Chapter 6

1. See William Dwight Whitney to Josiah Whitney, Jr., 30 October 1846, Yale Library, Whitney Collection (hereafter cited as YLW).

2. Josiah Whitney, Jr. to William Dwight Whitney, 25 April 1846, YLW.

3. William Dwight Whitney to Josiah Whitney, Jr., 30 June 1846, YLW.

4. William Dwight Whitney to Josiah Whitney, Jr., 31 July 1848, YLW.

5. William Dwight Whitney to F. J. Bumsted, 25 November 1849, YLW.

6. Idem., 6 January 1850, YLW.

7. Ibid.

8. William Dwight Whitney to Josiah Whitney, Sr., 11 January 1850, YLW.

9. William Dwight Whitney spent less than $600 a year in Germany, less than one-fourth the amount Theodore Woolsey had disbursed twenty years before.

10. William Dwight Whitney to Josiah Whitney, Sr., 11 January 1850, YLW.

11. Ibid.

12. Ibid.

13. MS diaries of William Dwight Whitney (hereafter cited as Whitney Diary), 9 February 1851, YLW.

14. William Dwight Whitney to F. J. Bumsted, 10 December 1850, YLW. He appears to have used his commitment to scholarly work as an antidote: "I am far from a well man today, & seem to be getting into the same condition as in old times, before I went to New Haven & made a new man of myself." Whitney Diary, 5 November 1850.

15. Ibid., 1 January 1852.

16. Ibid., 7 January 1851.

17. William Dwight Whitney to F. J. Bumsted, 10 December 1850, YLW.

18. Whitney Diary, 25 January 1851.

19. Ibid. Whitney could be vicious in his personal and professional relations. Nirad Chauhuri, in his *Scholar Extraordinary: The Life of the*

Right Honourable Max Müller (London, 1974), p. 259, remarks concerning Whitney's longstanding feud with Max Müller: "It is impossible to explain the ferocity of Whitney on any scholarly grounds."

20. Josiah Whitney Sr. to William Dwight Whitney, 18 October 1850, YLW.

21. The Reverend Mr. Peabody of Portsmouth, N.H., so assured a prospective American student, Lodowick Billings, as the latter anxiously informed William Dwight Whitney, 22 July 1850, YLW.

22. William Dwight Whitney to Josiah Whitney, Sr., 25 November 1850, YLW. Whitney was a great favorite among the American students in Berlin, but he often regarded them with less pleasure, on numerous occasions confiding to his journal his impatience with the duties of sociability: "We have spent the evening at Mr. Fay's, with a party of Americans, two or three new ones among them, & not very promising specimens either. . . . Indeed I am beginning to conclude that the great majority of Americans in the city are thorough asses & that the fewer acquaintances we have among them the better" (25 October 1851). His opinion of most German students was even lower; see William Dwight Whitney to Josiah Whitney, Sr., 11 May 1851, YLW.

23. Thomas Chase to Clement Smith, 23 November 1865, Harvard Archives, Clement Smith Collection (hereafter cited as HAS).

24. *German Universities: A Narrative of Personal Experience* (New York, 1874), p. 160.

25. W. W. Goodwin to Clement Smith, 7 August 1865, HAS.

26. For an account of a Christmas celebration at the Krone, see Samuel Fiske, *Mr. Dunn Browne's Experiences in Foreign Parts* (Boston, 1857), pp. 86–88.

27. Clement Smith Diary, 12 September 1865, HAS.

28. Hart, p. 160.

29. Ibid., p. 158.

30. W. W. Goodwin to Clement Smith, 7 August 1865, HAS. Goodwin also gave detailed advice on what to study and with whom.

31. C. A. Joy to William Dwight Whitney, 19 September 1851, YLW.

32. William Dwight Whitney to C. A. Joy, 5 October 1851, YLW.

33. Ibid.

34. C. A. Joy to William Dwight Whitney, 15 October 1851, YLW.

35. Clement Smith to Mrs. Henry Wood, 24 January 1866, HAS.

36. Clement Smith Diary, 11 September 1865, HAS.

37. William Dwight Whitney to Josiah Whitney, Jr., 24 October 1851, YLW.

38. Clement Smith to Mrs. Henry Wood, 24 January 1866, HAS.

39. White describes the Ranke seminar: "The lectures of Ranke, the most eminent of German historians, I could not follow. He had a habit

of becoming so absorbed in his subject, as to slide down in his chair, hold his finger up toward the ceiling, and then, with eye fastened on the tip of it, to go mumbling through a kind of rhapsody, which most of my fellow German students confessed they could not understand. It was a comical sight: half a dozen students crowding around his desk, listening as priests might listen to the sybil [*sic*] on her tripod, the other students being scattered around the room, in various stages of discouragement." *The Autobiography of Andrew Dickson White* (New York, 1905), p. 39.

40. Hall records that the principal benefits of his stay were a relaxed attitude toward the Sabbath, a fondness for a glass or two of beer, a liking for the company of (respectable) women, and a more tolerant religious belief. *The Life and Confessions of a Psychologist* (New York, 1923), pp. 218–22.

41. Clement Smith Diary, 18 April 1866, HAS.

42. Clement Smith to Mrs. Henry Wood, 13 December 1865, HAS.

43. Hart, p. 25.

44. Clement Smith Diary, 14 April 1866, HAS.

45. See his letters to Emerson, Houghton Library, Autograph Collection.

46. He got up at 6 A.M. and was working for all but three hours of his sixteen-hour day, according to his schedule; Clement Smith to his father, 29 March 1866, HAS.

47. *An historical discourse pronounced before the graduates of Yale College, 14 August 1850* (New Haven, 1850).

48. Hall, p. 182.

49. Francis Child to William Dwight Whitney, 22 June 1851, YLW.

Conclusion

1. *The Higher Learning in America* (New York, 1968), p. 3.

2. Ibid.

3. Ibid., p. 4.

4. Ibid.

5. See Georg Iggers, "The Image of Ranke in American and German Historical Thought," *History and Theory,* vol. 2, no. 1, pp. 17–20.

6. *The Works of Ralph Waldo Emerson,* ed. J. E. Cabot (Boston, 1883), 1:82.

7. "The Art of Life," *The Dial* 1 (1840):183.

Bibliographical Notes

General

We have libraries on the history of universities but very little historical work on the social and intellectual forms of modern scholarship. There is nothing like Thomas Kuhn's speculative but brilliant hypothesizing in his *The Structure of Scientific Revolutions* (Chicago, 1970). Some older scholars have given valuable suggestions, however. Ernst Cassirer's *The Problem of Knowledge: Philosophy, Science, and History since Hegel* (New Haven, 1952) and his *The Logic of the Humanities* (New Haven, 1961) offer many fruitful ideas for further work, as do Hajo Holborn's essays in *History and the Humanities* (New Haven, 1972) and Karl Mannheim in his *Essays on the Sociology of Knowledge* (New York, 1952).

John Merz, *A History of European Thought in the Nineteenth Century* (New York, 1965), 4 vols., gives a detailed survey of the growth of European knowledge throughout the nineteenth century. Helmut Plessner's essay "Zur Soziologie der modernen Forschung und ihrer Organization in der deutschen Universitäten," in his *Diesseits der Utopie* (Hamburg, 1968), offers some thoughtful suggestions for approaching this vast subject. R. Steven Turner's "The Prussian Universities and the Research Imperative" (Ph.D. diss., Princeton University, 1973) is an extremely helpful institutional history of the new form of scholarship. Joseph Ben-David and Awraham Zloczower, in "Universities and Academic Systems in Modern Societies," *European Journal of Sociology* 3 (1962: 64-68, provide a good introduction to the sociology of higher learning.

Chapter 1

Neuhumanismus is something of an unknown movement despite the prolific output of most of the German classical philologists of the eighteenth century. Many works, such as those of J. M. Gesner, are either impossible or difficult to obtain in the United States, and very few have been translated from the Latin. Most of Christian Gottlob Heyne's works are available, however. His *Sammlung antiquarisches Aufsätze* (Leipzig, 1778) gives an example of his scholarly work in German, while his "Verbesserungsvorschlage zur Hebung des Pädagogii zu Ilfeld," in the *Mitteilungen des Gesellschaft für deutsche Erzeihungs- und Schulgeschichte,* vol. 4 (1894), offers some of his educational ideas. Winckelmann's works are even more readily available in the original and in translation. Three of the latter are: *History of Ancient Art* (New York, 1969); *Writings on Art,* selected and translated by D. Irwin (London, 1972); and *Reflections on the Painting and Sculpture of the Greeks* (London, 1765).

Almost everything that Herder and Humboldt wrote touches the central concerns of *Neuhumanismus.* Herder's prize essay, *Abhandlung über den Ursprung der Sprache* (Berlin, 1772) and his *Älteste Urkunde des Menschengeschlects* Riga, 1774) are two important expressions of his ideas on language. Humboldt's "Über das Studium des Altertums und des griechischen in besondere," *Gesammelte Schriften* (Berlin, 1903–36), vol. 1; *Über die Aufgabe des Geschichteschreibers* (Berlin, 1821); and his *Linguistic Variability and Intellectual Development,* translated by George C. Buck and Frithjof A. Raven (Coral Gables, Fla., 1971), are important statements of his linguistic thought. Marianne Cowan's translations in *Humanist without Portfolio* (Detroit, 1963) provide a useful topical anthology which includes some of Humboldt's educational ideas. F. A. Wolf's educational writings were collected and edited by Wilhelm Körte in *Über Erziehung, Schule und Universität* (Leipzig, 1835).

Virtually the only general secondary source on *Neuhumanismus* is in vol. 2 of Friedrich Paulsen's *Geschichte des gelehrten Unterrichts auf den deutschen Schulen and Universitäten,* 2d edition (Leipzig, 1897). Leonard Krieger, in *The German Idea of Freedom* (Boston, 1957), and Georg Iggers, in *The German Conception of History* (Middletown, Conn., 1968), give valuable background to late eighteenth- and early nineteenth-century German thought. Hans Aarsleff, in *The Study of Language in England, 1780–1860* (Princeton, 1967) is the best general introduction to the history of philology in this period. John Sandys's epic *History of Classical Scholarship,* 3 vols. (Cambridge, 1908) provides a wealth of information. Holger Pedersen's *The Discovery of Language: Linguistic Science in the Nineteenth Century,* translated by J. W. Spargo (Bloomington, Ind., 1962) is also indispensable. There is an indisputable need for more analytic approaches. R. H. Robins provides some in his sketchy *A Short History of Linguistics* (London, 1967). Apart from these three secondary sources, historians of nineteenth-century philology will themselves have to wade into Friedrich Ast's *Grundriss der Philologie* (Landshut, 1808) and August Boeckh's pupils' compendium of his lectures in *Encyklopaedie und Methodologie der philologischen Wissenschaften* (Leipzig, 1877), two comprehensive surveys of philology at the beginning and middle of the nineteenth century, respectively. J. P. Pritchard has translated a small part of the *Encyklopaedie* in *On Interpretation* (Norman, Okla., 1968). Nirad Chaudhuri's *Scholar Extraordinary: The Life of the Rt. Honourable Friedrich Max Müller* (London, 1974) is genial but unhelpful.

Chapter 2

F. A. Wolf and the history of the Homeric question have remained as unstudied by historians as *Neuhumanismus* and philology. Most of Wolf's works are available in the United States, however. His *Prolegomena ad Homerum sive de operum Homericum* went through at least six editions in the nineteenth century. A German translation by Dr. Hermann Muchau (Leipzig, 1908) is virtually the only one available in a modern Western language. S. Reiz has edited a useful collection of Wolf's letters, *F. A. Wolf: Ein Leben in Briefen* (Stuttgart, 1935), and there was a full but biased biography by Wolf's student, Wilhelm Körte, *Lebens und Studium F. A. Wolf des Philologen,* 2 vols. (Essen, 1833).

Wolf's two predecessors in Homeric interpretation have not fared as well. Thomas Blackwell's *Enquiry into the Life and Writings of Homer* (Edinburgh, 1735) and Robert Wood's *Essay on the Original Genius of Homer,* 3d edition (London, 1824) are readily available—but that is all; they are not well studied. J. A. Davison, in his two essays, "The Homeric Question" and "The Homeric Text," in A. J. C Wace and F. H. Stubbings, ed., *A Companion to Homer* (New York, 1962), however, gives an invaluable introduction to the Homeric question. Richard Volkmann's *Geschichte und Kritik der Wolfschen Prolegomena zu Homer* (Leipzig, 1874), though old, offers more detail and analysis. Norman Cullan's comprehensive introduction to Pope's translation of the *Iliad* in the Twickenham edition of Alexander Pope's *Poems,* edited by Maynard Mack, vol. 7 (New Haven, 1967), is an admirable treatment of Homer's place in the early eighteenth century. Donald Foerster, *Homer in English Criticism* (New Haven, 1947) and M. C. Clark, *Greek Studies in England* (Cambridge, 1945) are also useful. Humphrey Trevalyan, *The Popular Background to Goethe's Hellenism* (New York, 1934), makes statements about the popularity of Homer which are refuted by his own figures. Hugh Honour has some thoughtful remarks on Homer and the Greek revival in relation to the cult of Ossian in his *Neoclassicism* (Baltimore, 1973). Harry Hatfield's *Aesthetic Paganism in German Literature* (Cambridge, Mass., 1964) is the best study of the Greek revival in Germany.

Chapter 3

There is no satisfactory secondary source on the American students in the German universities. Jurgen Herbst, *The German Historical School in American Scholarship* (Ithaca, N.Y., 1969), centers on the post-Civil War period and relies largely on secondary sources for the first seven decades of the nineteenth century. Lawrence Veysey, *The Emergence of the American University* (Chicago, 1965), also centers on the later period, though there is a great deal of material on the context of American educational thought in the earlier period. Henry Pochmann, *German Culture in America: Philosophical and Literary Influences, 1600-1900* (Madison, Wis., 1957), has the best general account of Americans abroad in Germany, though the only primary materials consulted seem to have been the well-worn manuscripts of Ticknor, Everett, Bancroft, and Cogswell. Richard Barnes, "German Influences on American Historical Studies, 1884-1914" (Ph.D. diss., Yale University, 1953), also has a chapter on the Americans who studied in Germany but adds very little that is new. Charles Thwing, *The German and the American University: One Hundred Years of History* (New York, 1928), claims familiarity with unpublished statistics and sources, but contains no substantiation and repeats much of what Daniel B. Shumway wrote in the introduction to his exhaustive list of Americans who studied in Germany, "Göttingen's American Students," *German-American Review,* vol. 3 (June, 1907), a source that has not yet been fully exploited. Besides this enumeration, it is possible to gather more names of Americans from Burke Hinsdale's short list in his "Note on the History of Foreign Influence upon Education in the United States," United States Bureau of Education, *Reports of the Commissioner* 1 (1897-98):591-632.

Several German universities published lists of their matriculants in the nineteenth century, and it is possible to comb through them looking for Americans; the place of birth is almost invariably recorded. I have managed to do this only incompletely for Heidelberg, from *Die Matrikel der Universität Heidelberg* (Heidelberg, 1884-1916). Father's occupation and previous place of study are sometimes recorded as well. But where they are not, and where names are culled from other sources, much more work is needed to obtain this and other data. *The Dictionary of American Biography* is an obvious place to start. Other biographical encyclopedias, like *Appleton's* include many additional names. Since there were many fewer colleges in the period before 1870, college catalogues (which almost invariably in this period recorded the names of their students) tracked down a great many. Many colleges have also published their alumni records, including: *Historical Register of Yale University, 1701-1937* (New Haven, 1939); *Quinquennial Catalogue of the Officers and Graduates of Harvard University, 1636-1930* (Cambridge, Mass., 1930); *Amherst College Biographical Record 1963* (Amherst, 1963); *Columbia University Alumni Record,* 1754-1931 (New York, 1932); *Princeton University Alumni Directory* (Princeton, 1888-); and George Chapman, *Sketches of the Alumni of Dartmouth College* (Cambridge, Mass., 1867)—to name only the most useful. Other published histories and necrologies also provided information, including: *Obituary Record of the Graduates of Yale College* (New Haven, 1860-1910); Franklin Dexter, *Biographical*

Notices of the Graduates of Yale College (New Haven, 1913); and James
Harold Easterby, *A History of the College of Charleston, founded in 1770*
(Charleston, S.C., 1935), and *The History of the College of William and
Mary, 1660–1874* (Richmond, Va., 1874), both of which provide compre-
hensive lists of their graduates.

Specific college histories, too numerous to mention, can also give
biographical data, especially on faculty and prominent alumni. For accounts of the German university system, Steven Turner (cited above in
the General section) gives the best account of the creation of the modern
German university. Friedrich Paulsen, *The German Universities and
University Study,* translated by Frank Tilly (New York, 1906), is still
useful, and since I did not have the benefit of Turner's dissertation for
this chapter, J. Conrad, *The German Universities for the Last Fifty Years,*
translated by John Hutchinson (Glasgow, 1885), and Wilhelm Lexis,
Das Unterrichtswesen in Deutschen Reich, 4 vols. (Berlin, 1904), were
useful, especially for their statistical tables.

Chapter 4

The primary sources for the first four Americans to study in the German
universities are well known and well used. Bancroft's papers in the Massachusetts Historical Society are particularly interesting, though they have
been so heavily used that they must be microfilmed soon. The Everett
Collection there is already on microfilm. The Ticknor diaries in the Dartmouth College library are also on microfilm, though much less useful
than the other collections: Ticknor was too guarded to give himself away
as often as Bancroft or Cogswell. The Bancroft papers in the Cornell
library pertain mainly to a later period than that of his German study.
But there are some fascinating letters from his family, particularly his
brother and mother, that would provide a certain amount of evidence
for a venturesome psychohistorian. Bancroft's notebooks in the New
York Public Library could also be much better used than they have been
to date. The Kirkland papers in the Harvard Archives are messy and ill-
arranged, but the bound volumes of the Harvard College Papers there
contain many useful documents. Joseph Cogswell's letters in the Harvard
Archives, the Massachusetts Historical Society, and the New York Public
Library have all been examined repeatedly, though there is still material
for a careful psychological study. Theodore Dwight Woolsey's papers in
the Yale Manuscripts and Archives are a vast source which I regret not
having used more fully. Henry Dwight's papers are unfortunately very
limited.

The secondary sources for these first Americans in the German universities are almost as vast as the manuscript holdings. Russell Nye, *George*

Bancroft: Brahmin Rebel (New York, 1944), is a useful biography. David Tyack's *George Ticknor and the Boston Brahmins* (Cambridge, Mass., 1967) is solid and helpful, as is Orie Long, *Literary Pioneers: The American Exploration of German Culture* (Cambridge, Mass., 1935). Cynthia Stokes Brown, though I disagree completely with her conclusions in "The American Discovery of the German University: Four Students in Göttingen, 1815-1822" (Ph.D. diss., Johns Hopkins University, 1966), provides a comprehensive and detailed account of the intellectual and social background of Göttingen at the time when the Americans arrived. She also has a full account of exactly what they studied and did, though she appears to have ignored completely their psychological problems. Thomas Wentworth Higginson's pioneering article, "Göttingen and Harvard Eighty Years Ago," *Harvard Graduates Magazine* 6 (1897): 6-18, reprints some interesting letters but offers no serious analysis. George Ticknor's *Life, Letters and Journals* (Boston, 1876) and *The Life and Letters of George Bancroft,* edited by M. A. deWolfe Howe (New York, 1908), have been superceded as a research source by all of the work that has been done with the manuscripts.

Chapter 5

A good history of classical scholarship in the United States does not yet exist. Frederick Rudolph's all-purpose survey, *The American College and University, A History* (New York, 1962), provides material on the fight over the classical curriculum. See George P. Schmidt, *The Liberal Arts College: A Chapter in American Cultural History* (New Brunswick, N.J., 1957), for a discussion of this controversy. The two major documents of the curriculum fight are *The Yale Report of 1828* and Francis Brown's *Thoughts on the Present Collegiate System in the United States* (Boston, 1842). Russell Nye's new book, *Society and Culture in America, 1830-1860* (New York, 1974), provides a more balanced and recent cultural history of the period than Van Wyck Brooks, *The Flowering of New England, 1815-1865* (New York, 1937), or Vernon Parrington, *Main Currents in American Thought,* vol. 2: *The Romantic Revolution in America, 1800-1860.* The volumes of the *North American Review* constitute one primary source for classical scholarship in this period, since many serious works of classical philology from England or America were reviewed, often in great detail. Many German and French works of classical scholarship were also noticed. As for American classical scholarship of this period, almost all of it consists of editions. One of these which precipitated great controversy was C. C. Felton's *The Agamemnon of Aeschylus* (Boston, 1847).

Chapter 6

Because so few American students left substantial diaries or correspondence relating to their German study, I have had to rely principally on two major sources for this chapter: the William Dwight Whitney Manuscripts in the Yale Library and the Clement Smith Collection in the Harvard Archives. The Whitney collection is a vast treasure-house that has been too little exploited. His meticulously kept diaries indicate where he was and what he studied virtually every single day of his adult life. Since he studied in Berlin in the winters and Tübingen in the summers, his letters to Professors Weber and Roth of those two universities, respectively, provide an exact chronicle of his initiation into Sanskrit scholarship. Clement Smith's diaries and notebooks were also helpful, though his correspondence was neither as full nor as interesting as that of Whitney. The Justin Winsor papers in the Harvard Archives were so badly kept as to be almost useless. The papers of Francis Child and George Lane were not extensive enough to provide much help.

I relied as well on a number of printed accounts of American students in German universities, most notably James Morgan Hart, *German Universities: A Narrative of Personal Experience* (New York, 1874), and G. Stanley Hall's *Life and Confessions of a Psychologist* (New York, 1923). Lawrence Veysey (cited above) and Richard Storrs, *The Beginnings of Higher Education in America* (Chicago, 1953), along with Frederick Rudolph (cited above) provide the best guides to the emergence of the American university system.

Index

Adams, John, 109

Allen, William Francis, 116

Angell, James Burrill, 115

Ast, Friedrich, 24–26

Bancroft, George: mentioned passim; perception of F. A. Wolf, 71–73; relationship with John Kirkland, 72–91, 92, 94–100; relationship with Edward Everett, 79–87; on the use of the classics, 103–04

Beecher, Henry Ward, 141

Berlin University: as model of a German university, 9; enrollments of Americans in, 55, 57–61, 155–58. *See also* Colleges and Universities, American; Students

Bildung: relationship to *Neuhumanismus,* 18–20

Blackwell, Thomas, 36–39, 45

Boeckh, August, 24, 26, 76

Bopp, Franz, 127

Bristed, Charles, 108, 178n19

Cabot, James Eliot, 112

Calvert, George, 111–12

Camp, Clinton, 133

Campbell, Duncan, 116

Career patterns, academic, 66–69, 117, 152–53, 174–75n68, n60

Chase, Thomas, 130–31

Child, Francis, 67, 131, 141–42, 151

Classical philology. *See* Philology, classical

Classical revival. *See* Greek revival

Cogswell, Joseph Green: men-

tioned, 2, 51, 96, 177n88; experience in Germany, 92

Colleges and universities, American: graduates who studied in Germany, 62–65, 159–61. *See also* Harvard University; Students; Yale University

Curtius, Ernst, 138–39

Dacier, Mme. A. L., 34

Dissen, G. L., 77, 95

Dwight, Henry, 93–94, 102, 151

Eichhorn, J. G., 75, 95, 99–100

Eliot, Charles, 116

Emerson, Ralph Waldo, 151, 177–78n5

Ernesti, J. A., 14, 17, 35

Everett, Edward: mentioned passim; perception of F. A. Wolf, 71–72; work in America, 73; relationship with Moses Stuart, 74–75; experience in Germany, 76–79; relationship with George Bancroft, 79–87, 94, 95, 104, 111

Faculties, divisions of German universities: enrollment of Americans in, 51–59, 155–58. *See also* Colleges and universities, American; Law; Medicine; Philosophy; Students; Theology

Furness, Horace Howard, 67, 151

Gesner, J. M., 14, 17

Gildersleeve, Basil, 115, 151

Gilman, Daniel Coit, 51, 115

Goethe, J. W. von, 46–47